MW01487169

BLACK PEOPLE & THEIR PLACE IN WORLD HISTORY

9/21/02
Best wishes,
Leroy Vaughn

Leroy William Vaughn, MD, MBA

Willie "C" Jackson
1531 W. 64th Street
Los Angeles CA. 90047

Black People And
Their Place In World History
First printing 2002
Copyright © 2002 by Leroy William Vaughn, MD, MBA

All Rights Reserved under International and Pan-American Copyright Conventions.
No part of this book may be reproduced or transmitted in any form or by any means,
electronic or mechanical, including photocopy, recording, or any information storage
and retrieval system, without prior permission in writing from Dr. Leroy William
Vaughn. All inquiries should be addressed to 323 North Prairie Avenue, Suite 217,
Inglewood, CA 90301.

ISBN: 0-9715920-0-4
Printed in the United States

Cover design and book formatting by Mary Lewis

THIS BOOK IS DEDICATED TO:
MY LOVING MOTHER, FATHER, AND BROTHER
AND
MY WONDERFUL, CARING STAFF

FOREWARD BY BRAD PYE JR.

Leroy William Vaughn M.D., M.B.A. is not only one of the world's renowned ophthalmologists, but also one of the leading authorities on Black history. Basketball is Michael Jordan's game. Black history and ophthalmology are Dr. Vaughn's games. Dr. Vaughn's medical credentials and expertise as a diabetic eye specialist and as a remarkable surgeon make him one of the leading practitioners in his field. His knowledge as an historian is equally as outstanding.

Dr. Vaughn's patients swear by him for his medical skills. Historians marvel at him because of his talents as a researcher and writer on the subject of Black history. As a lecturer, he's one of the most in-demand speakers in the nation. Like magic, Dr. Vaughn can rattle off facts on Black history like an orator recites a speech he has practiced on delivering for days. When it comes to reciting the roles Black people have played in world history, Dr. Vaughn has dazzled some of the most learned minds in America.

Confirmation of this fact can be found on the pages of this in-depth study on the subject. For instance, did you know that a Black man with only a sixth grade education, named Garrett Morgan (1875-1963), invented the first traffic signal, the gas mask, and marketed the G.A. Morgan Refining Cream, which was the first hair straightening product? Did you know that Garrett Morgan made so much money from his hair cream that he was able to purchase an automobile? In fact, traffic congestion while driving his new car was motivation for Morgan's traffic signal invention.

Did you know that in 1721 an African slave, named Onesimus, taught his "master" the age-old African technique for smallpox inoculation in which a pustule from an infected person was ruptured with a thorn and then used to puncture the skin of a non-infected person? Did anyone ever tell you that the original Haitians were called the Arawaks, or Tainos, before Christopher Columbus and that they were very generous and could swim long distances? Did you know that George Franklin Grant, a Black man, invented the golf tee in 1898 and patented it a year later? Grant, one of the first two African American graduates of the Harvard Dental School, took a liking to golf. He invented the golf tee because he didn't like the way golfers had to mix dirt and water to make a mud mound for teeing off. Did anyone ever tell you that a Black man named John Lee Love invented the Love Pencil Sharpener in 1897, the kind most first-graders take to school today?

Did anyone ever tell you that Dr. Charles Richard Drew was the discoverer of successful blood plasma storage techniques that made blood banks possible? In 1941, the American Red Cross appointed Dr. Drew as director of its first blood bank. Did anyone ever tell you that the collective contributions of Black Americans to science is so extensive that it is not possible to live a full day in any part of the United States, or the world for that matter, without sharing in the benefits of their contributions in such fields as: biology, chemistry, physics, space and nuclear science? Well, if you didn't know these things, then keep on reading, and Dr. Vaughn will tell you about these and hundreds of other facts about Black history.

Other inventions patented by African Americans include the folding lawn chair, the doorstop, the ironing board with collapsible legs, and the bottle cap. In fact, there's a long list of inventions made by Blacks during an age dominated by Whites. If Michael Jordan, Magic Johnson, Shaquille O'Neal, Kobe Bryant, and Elgin Baylor had been born in the 18th or 19th century, we would never have known their names because of a concerted effort not to acknowledge the accomplishments of Black people.

Dr. Vaughn didn't just decide to write a book on Black history. This has been his passion and his life's mission! Academically, Dr. Vaughn has the knowledge and the talents to make his life's work a reality on the pages of this book. Dr. Vaughn was rooted and grounded in Black history as a student at Morehouse College in Atlanta, where he obtained a Bachelor of Science degree and graduated Phi Beta Kappa in 1969, after a two-year premedical study tour at the University of Vienna in Austria.

In addition to Dr. Vaughn, Morehouse College has produced some of the most prominent and learned scholars in the world including Dr. Martin Luther King Jr., U.S. Surgeon General Dr. David Satcher, and Dr. Charles Finch. Dr. Benjamin Mays, one of the world's most noted educators and a mentor to Dr. King, was president of Morehouse College from 1950 until 1967, and set an extremely high standard for all Morehouse graduates.

Medically speaking, Dr. Vaughn is tops in his field. He received his medical degree from Wayne State University in Detroit, where he also received the Franklin C. McLean Award in 1972, as the most outstanding Black medical student in the nation. He interned at the Department of Medicine in Chapel Hill, NC, and completed his Ophthalmology fellowship and research training at Harvard University's Massachusetts Eye and Ear Hospital in 1979. Dr. Vaughn was certified as a Diplomate of the American Board of Ophthalmology in 1978, after scoring in the top three percentile nationally on the written examination. Moreover, he was named as an Associate Examiner for the American Board of Ophthalmology's oral examinations in 1984.

In addition to being a brilliant scholar, Dr. Vaughn is also a community leader. For giving his time and his talents to the community, he was honored by the late Los Angeles Mayor Tom Bradley, L.A. County Supervisor Kenneth Hahn, the State of California, and the Aesculapian Honorary Society.

Dr. Vaughn's book should not only be required reading for Blacks, but for all people. Most of society still believes what historian Arnold Toynbee wrote in his 1934 history book: "It will be seen that when we classify mankind by color, the only primary race that has not made a creative contribution to any civilization is the Black race." Dr. Vaughn sets the record straight on this lie, and on so many other untruths about Black history.

Vernon E. Jordan, better known as a civil rights fighter, businessman, lawyer, and "first friend" of President Bill Clinton, vividly illustrates the essence of Dr. Vaughn's book when he wrote in his book entitled <u>Vernon Can Read! A Memoir</u>: "Black people have done wonderful things for this country (saved its soul, in fact), and we have been an example to the world in the process. That should never be forgotten, even as we continue to press ahead, in our many and varied ways, toward our future. If we did so much when we had so little, think of what we can do now that we have so much more."

Covered in Dr. Vaughn's book are the ancient period, after Christ, after 1492 (Columbus), after 1776 (Independence), after 1865 (slavery), and after 1900 (20th Century). If you really want to know about "Black People and Their Place in World History", then you should rush out and obtain a copy of Dr. Vaughn's masterpiece, before the sun goes down.

Brad Pye, Jr.
Formerly (for thirty years):
    Los Angeles Sentinel Newspaper's Sports Editor
    Sports Director for KGFJ, KACE, KJLH, and KDAY radio stations
Currently Sports columnist for the following publications:
    Los Angeles Watts Times
    Compton Bulletin
    Inglewood Today
    Inland News

CONTENTS

CONTENTS

World War II Black soldier recruiting poster

WHO CREATED CIVILIZATION?

President Thomas Jefferson said, "Never yet could I find that a Black had uttered a thought above the level of plain narration...never saw an elementary tract of painting or sculpture." Congressman Thomas Hardwick of Georgia, in 1904, demanded and received the disenfranchisement of Black people from the gains made after the Civil War. He said, "Black people never founded a government nor made a single step toward civilization that did not soon lapse in barbarism, except under the fostering care and guidance of White people." Historian Arnold Toynbee wrote in his 1934 history book: "It will be seen that when we classify mankind by color, the only primary race that has not made a creative contribution to any civilization is the Black race."

Former President Richard Nixon was quoted in the Haldeman Diary as stating, "the Black race is the only race, which never founded a civilization." Scientist and Professor R. B. Carrell concludes, "Savages, including the whole Negro race, should on account of their low mentality and unpleasant nature be painlessly exterminated." Were White scholars and presidents never taught the correct version of history, or has there been a conspiracy for the past 200 years to deny Black civilizations? Before Greece, Rome or Europe were ever established, there were multiple Black civilizations throughout the world, which were already thousands of years old.

All of the elements of civilization first began in Africa, including religion, art, science, government, mining, writing, mathematics, architecture, engineering, and agriculture. Dr. Charles Nelson at the University of Massachusetts states that animal domestication occurred in Kenya 15,000 years ago; and that agricultural sites have been carbon dated in Egypt to 18,000 BC.

The oldest numeration system was found in Zaire by Dr. Jean de Heinzelin with markings on the Ishango Bone dated 8000 BC. She also said that the people were

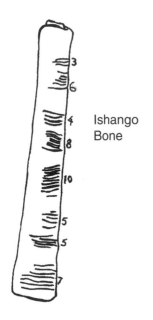

Ishango Bone

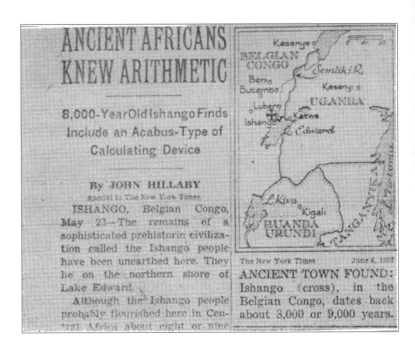

ANCIENT AFRICANS KNEW ARITHMETIC

8,000-Year Old Ishango Finds Include an Acabus-Type of Calculating Device

By JOHN HILLABY
Special to The New York Times

ISHANGO, Belgian Congo, May 23—The remains of a sophisticated prehistoric civilization called the Ishango people have been unearthed here. They lie on the northern shore of Lake Edward.

Although the Ishango people probably flourished here in Central Africa about eight or nine

The New York Times   June 6, 1957
ANCIENT TOWN FOUND: Ishango (cross), in the Belgian Congo, dates back about 8,000 or 9,000 years.

familiar with prime numbers and multiplication by two, since the markings were paired at 3-6, 4-8, and 5-10.

Astronomy and astrology are believed to have existed for almost 50,000 years. The oldest stellar calendar is dated 4241 BC. It has 365 1/4 days and 12 months with 30 days in each month. The ancient Africans were also the first to divide the day into 24 hours and to begin the day at midnight.

African medical textbooks have been found that are over 5,000 years old. Ancient Africans were very well versed in medical diagnosis and treatment with as many as 1,000 animal, plant, and mineral products used in the treatment of illness.

All religions are believed to have originated in Africa, including Hinduism, Buddhism, Christianity, and Islam. General Massey states that the religious records of all religions including the Christian Bible are traceable and in many

Advanced Architecture and Engineering

cases are direct copies of the religious records of ancient Egypt and Nubia. St. Augustine, one of the founding fathers of Christian Theology, wrote, "What is now called the Christian religion has existed among the ancients and was not absent from the beginning of the human race."

Hieroglyphics

The ancient Black Egyptians created paper about 4000 BC, which made the recording of history and science more practical for library storage. It is estimated that over 700,000 books were in the libraries of Egypt before Homer, the father of Western literature, was even born.

Could it be that Black history is the best kept secret in the world or have politicians, including past presidents, denied Black history to accelerate Black disenfranchisement?

REFERENCES AND ADDITIONAL READING

Ben-Jochannan, Y.A. (1970) <u>African Origins of the Major Western Religions.</u> Baltimore: Black Classic Press.

Ben-Jochannan, Y.A. (1988) <u>Africa: Mother of Western Civilization</u>. Baltimore, MD

Browder, A. (1992) <u>Nile Valley Contributions to Civilization</u>. Washington, D C: The Institute of Karmic Guidance.

Budge, E.A. (1967) <u>The Egyptian Book of the Dead</u>. New York: Dover Publications.

Diop, C.A. (1981) <u>The African Origin of Civilization: Myth or Reality</u>. Westport Connecticut: Lawrence Hill and Co.

Finch, C. (1991) <u>Echoes of the Old Darkland.</u> Decatur, Georgia: Khenti, Inc.

Finch, C. (1990) <u>The African Background to Medical Science</u>. London, UK: Billing and Sons Ltd.

Haldeman, H. (1994) <u>The Haldeman Diaries: Inside the Nixon White House</u>. New York: Berkley Publishing Group.

James, G. (1954) <u>Stolen Legacy</u>. San Francisco: Julian Richardson.

Khamit-Kush, I. (1983) <u>What They Never Told You in History Class</u>. Bronx, NY Luxorr Publications.

Massey, G. (1970) <u>Ancient Egypt</u>. New York: Samuel Weiser.

Massey, G. (1883) <u>Natural Genesis</u>. London: Williams and Norgate.

Rogers, J. (1991) <u>Africa's Gift to America.</u> St. Petersburg, Florida: Helga Rogers Publishing.

Van Sertima, I. (ed.) (1991) <u>Blacks in Science</u>. New Brunswick, New Jersey: Transaction Books.

HATSHEPSUT

Hatshepsut of ancient Egypt is considered the greatest female ruler of all time. This Black empress is the first woman in recorded history to challenge and destroy the theory of male supremacy. After fighting her way to power, she held the throne of the world's mightiest empire at that time for 34 years. Since her father, Thutmose I had conquered most of the known world, Hatshepsut was not faced with an external enemy. Her greatest nemeses were the priests of the God Amen who were determined not to end more than 3000 years of masculine tradition.

Hatshepsut as a sphinx with Pharaoh's false beard

When the priests demanded that she step aside and allow her brother Thutmose II to rule as pharaoh, Hatshepsut tried to discredit her half brother by announcing that Thutmose II was the son of Mutnefert, a concubine, and therefore royal blood was only passed through to her. She knew that all Black African societies including Egypt were matrilineal, which means that inheritance, including the power of the throne, was passed through the female line. Hatshepsut could easily trace her female ancestry to her jet-Black Ethiopian grandmother, Nefertari-Aahmes, but faced with the alternatives of possible civil war or compromise, she agreed to marry

5

Thutmose II. By all accounts, however, Thutmose II was an overweight, sickly, weakling and allowed Hatshepsut to run the affairs of the monarchy unopposed during their 13 years of marriage (1492-1479 BC). Upon the death of Thutmose II, Hatshepsut startled the nation by boldly announcing that she was a man. She donned a fake beard, male clothes, and changed her name from Hatshepsitu to Hatshepsut, its male equivalent. This would be similar to changing one's female name from Demetria to the male version of Demetrius. Hatshepsut crushed all further opposition by also announcing that she was not the daughter of Thutmose I, but the virgin birth son of God Amen and her mother Ahmose. She declared that the great God Amen appeared to her mother "in a flood of light and perfume" and by "Immaculate Conception" this union produced a baby boy. For those in doubt, she had the entire bedroom scene painted on the walls of her temple in intimate detail. Thereafter, her sculptured portraits depicted her with a beard and male features. She also demanded that her title be changed to "King/Pharaoh of the North and South; the Horus of Gold; Conqueror of All Lands; the Mighty One."

These changes must have come as quite a shock to the priests who had witnessed her giving birth to two daughters, Nefrure and Merytra-Hatshepset, while married to Thutmose II. Several priests also joked that the one title she could not add was "Mighty Bull of Maat" which implies male fertility.

Hatshepsut became firmly established as King/Pharaoh for the next 21 years (1479-1458 BC), and her popularity increased tremendously as did the prosperity of Egypt. She was such a shrewd administrator, sending ambassadors to all her conquered lands, that gold tributes became so plentiful they no longer were weighed but measured in bushel baskets. J. A. Rogers wrote: "She began to publicize herself in the most sensational manner of that time, that is, by the building of temples, pyramids, and obelisks, the size and grandeur of which had never been seen before and regarded by the popular mind as a gauge of the ruler's power."

To further demonstrate her triumph over the priests of Amen, Hatshepsut commissioned her Black architect boyfriend, Senmut, to build a structure that would overshadow the colossal temple of Amen-Ra (Karnak), which was the stronghold of her opponents. Under Senmut's genius was created a magnificent temple, called Deir el Bahari, out of the sheer rock cliff that looks down on the temple of Amen-Ra.

The Temple of Hatshepsut called Deir el Bahari created from a rock cliff

It sits high in the cliffs with a frontage of 800 feet and a series of courtyards and colonnades decorated with reliefs, shrines, inscriptions, innumerable statues, wonderful terraces, and paradisiacal gardens. Deir el Bahari is still considered one of the world's most remarkable architectural specimens and the embodiment of Senmut's multifaceted genius. Hatshepsut lined the walkway to her temple with sandstone sphinxes of herself. Sphinx monuments were previously reserved only for the male as "Loving Horus".

Senmut, Architect of
Deir El Bahari

As a final blow to her detractors, Hatshepsut ordered the creation of two of the largest most beautiful rose granite obelisks the world had ever seen and presented them as gifts to the temple of Amen-Ra. Hatshepsut astutely ordered the obelisks taller than the temple so that the roof had to be removed to accommodate her gifts, despite the fact that this temple was one of the most colossal structures made by man. Hatshepsut made the obelisks even more conspicuous and overshadowing of the temple by encasing their tops with a precious gold-silver mixture. This made the obelisks so brilliant in sunlight that whenever a visitor looked out on the city, the most dazzling sight was no longer the temple of Amen-Ra but her obelisks.

By riding into battle with her troops, Hatshepsut was the forerunner to all the great African warrior queens from the Candaces of Ethiopia to Queen Nzinga of Angola. Although there were no major wars during her reign, there were revolts. One ancient scribe recounted Hatshepsut's military accomplishments during a Nubian revolt on a wall in Senmut's tomb: "I followed the 'Living Horus' (Hatshepsut) of upper and lower Egypt- may HE live forever! I saw when HE overthrew the Nubian Bowman, and when their chiefs were brought to HIM as living captives. I saw when HE razed Nubia, I being in HIS majesty's following..." Denoting Hatshepsut with masculine pronouns was demanded by her and was also a method used to exalt her position as "Living Horus".

Despite the fact that she often dressed as a male, she never lost touch with her feminine side. Scribes wrote that she was "lovely to look at; graceful in her movements, and fragrant as a flower." Hatshepsut wrote of herself: "My fragrance is like a divine breath; my scent reaches as far as the land of Punt; my skin is that of pure gold...I have no equal among the gods who were since the world was."

Hatshepsut's rule was one of the most prosperous times ever for the people of Egypt who had abundant work, shelter, and food. Memories of Hatshepsut persisted for many centuries after her reign and stories were passed down from generation to generation about her wonderful deeds, brave nature, beauty, and ingenuity until she reached godlike stature. Hatshepsut, a great Black leader of Africa's Golden Age, has been called "the first great woman in history" but in actuality may be "history's greatest woman".

REFERENCES AND ADDITIONAL READING

Breasted, J. (1937) <u>A History of Egypt</u>. New York: Charles Scribner's Sons.

Cottrell, L. (1961) <u>The Lost Pharaohs</u>. New York: The Universal Library.

Diop, C.A. (1978) <u>The Cultural Unity of Black Africa</u>. Chicago: Third World Press.

Hyman, M. (1994) <u>Blacks Before America</u>. Trenton, NJ: Africa World Press.

Montet, P. (1964) <u>Eternal Egypt</u>. New York: The New American Library.

Murnane, W. (1977) <u>Ancient Egyptian Coregencies</u>. Chicago: The Oriental Institute of the University of Chicago.

Murray, M. (1963) <u>The Splendor that was Egypt</u>. New York: Hawthorne Books.

Redford, D. (1967) <u>History and Chronology of the Eighteenth Dynasty of Egypt</u>. Toronto: University of Toronto Press.

Rogers, J.A. (1946) <u>World's Great Men of Color</u>. New York: Collier Books.

Romer, J. (1981) <u>Valley of the Kings</u>. New York: William Morrow and Co.

Sewell, B. (1968) <u>Egypt Under the Pharaohs</u>. New York: G.P. Putnam's Sons.

Sweetman, D. (1984) <u>Women Leaders in African History</u>. Portsmouth, NH: Heinemann Educational Books.

Van Sertima, I. (ed.) (1988) <u>Black Women in Antiquity</u>. New Brunswick, New Jersey: Transaction Publishers.

Wells, E. (1969) <u>Hatshepsut</u>. New York: Doubleday and Co.

Williams, C. (1987) <u>The Destruction of Black Civilization</u>. Chicago: Third World Press.

BLACK EGYPTIANS

The ancient Egyptians produced one of the highest forms of civilization ever known. They were outstanding in the fields of mathematics, astronomy and astrology, medicine, religion, philosophy, architecture, engineering, art, government, science, mining and virtually all other fields involving the elements of civilization.

In mathematics, the ancient Egyptians gave us not only arithmetic, but algebra, geometry, trigonometry, and also calculus. Higher math was needed for building temples and pyramids. The Egyptian Great Pyramid is among the seven Wonders of the World, and even today we could not reproduce this structure. Egyptian medical textbooks have been found that are over 5,000 years old, and many of their methods of diagnosis and treatment are still used today.

Gerald Massey states that the religious records of virtually all religions including the Christian bible, are traceable and in many cases, direct copies of the religious records of ancient Egypt. .J.A. Rogers says, "every Christian priest from Moses through Jesus was taught in the Egyptian mysteries system." Acts 7:22 in the Bible confirms that Moses was learned in the wisdom of the Egyptians. Every Greek philosopher and writer from Homer to Pythagoras and Aristotle are known to have studied in ancient Egypt. The Egyptians were also the first to produce paper and had over 700,000 books in their libraries when invaded by Alexander.

Given the outstanding accomplishments of the ancient Egyptians, it is understandable why every society on Earth has claimed the ancient Egyptians as their ancestors including: Arabs, Europeans, and Asians. However, the current Egyptian is as different from the ancient Egyptian as the current American is from the ancient American. Cheikh Anta Diop, a Senegalese professor and scientist, claims that the original ancient Egyptian civilization was built by Black Africans long before Egypt was invaded by Assyrians, Libyans, Persians, Greeks, Romans, and Arabs.

A Cairo symposium was held on February 3, 1974 by the United Nations Economic Social and Cultural Organization called (UNESCO) on the ethnicity of the ancient Egyptians. Diop convinced everyone in attendance that the ancient Egyptians were Black Africans based on his seven (7) point presentation. First, he developed a melanin dosage test and demonstrated that ancient Egyptian mummies had heavy doses of melanin in their skin, which was non-existent in White-skinned races. Second, he proved that ancient Egyptians had group B type blood, common among Africans, and not group A type blood, characteristic of the White race. Third, he gave osteological measurements of the skull and long bones

and demonstrated typical Negroid facial and bodily proportions among the Egyptians. Fourth, Diop produced records from ancient Greek and Latin writers, who were contemporary with the ancient Egyptians, including Herodotus, Aristotle, Lucian, and Diodorus. These writers all claimed that the ancient Egyptians, Ethiopians, and Colchidians all had Black skin, thick lips, kinky hair, and thin legs.

Pharaoh Namer 1st Dynasty

Pharaoh Akhenaten 18 th Dynasty
First to introduce Monotheism

Fifth, Diop showed artwork by ancient Egyptians who drew themselves with Black skin and wooly hair. They even named their country Kemit, which means *Black* and called themselves Kemites. Sixth, ancient Egyptian gods were all portrayed as jet-black in color and during this period most nations drew their deities in their own image. Seventh, circumcision is of African origin beginning before 4000 BC in Ethiopia and Egypt. Circumcision was not practiced in the rest of the world unless they were taught by the Egyptians.

Finally, there is a strong linguistic kinship or affinity between the ancient Egyptian language and the languages of Africa, especially the West African language of Wolof. These languages have many words, which are the same in sound and meaning.

Egyptian God Osiris

13

Cheikh Anta Diop was successful in convincing everyone at the 1974 UNESCO Symposium that the ancient Egyptians were Black Africans, and yet western society continues to portray them as White. The epitome of unconscionable cultural thievery is the pyramid shaped Luxor hotel in Las Vegas, that displays White Egyptian figures inside, and a Sphinx outside with blue eyes and a European nose.

REFERENCES AND ADDITIONAL READING

Bernal, M. (1987) <u>Black Athena</u>. London: Free Association Books.

Diop, C.A. (1978) <u>The Cultural Unity of Black Africa</u>. Chicago: Third World Press.

Diop, C.A. (1981) <u>The African Origin of Civilization: Myth or Reality</u>. Westport Connecticut: Lawrence Hill and Co.

Diop, C.A. (1981) "The Origin of the Ancient Egyptians" in Mokhtar, G. (ed.) <u>General History of Africa.</u> Berkeley: University of California Press.

Diop, C.A. (1991) <u>Civilization or Barbarism.</u> Westport Connecticut: Lawrence Hill and Co.

Greenburg, J.H. (1963) <u>The Languages of Africa</u>. Bloomington, Indiana: Indiana Press.

Herodotus. (1983) <u>The Histories</u>. Middlesex, U.K.: Penguin Books.

James, G. (1954) <u>Stolen Legacy.</u> San Francisco: Julian Richardson.

Massey, G. (1970) <u>Ancient Egypt</u>. New York: Samuel Weiser.

Massey, G. (1883) <u>Natural Genesis</u>. London: Williams and Norgate.

St. Clair, D. (1987) <u>Black Folk Here and There.</u> Los Angeles: UCLA.

Van Sertima, I. (ed.) (1989) <u>Egypt Revisited</u>. New Brunswick, New Jersey: Transaction Publishers.

Van Sertima, I. (ed.) (1986) <u>Great African Thinkers.</u> New Brunswick, New Jersey: Transaction Publishers.

ANCIENT BLACK NUBIANS IN AMERICA

Pharaoh Taharqa who is mentioned in the Bible ruled over Egypt and Nubia from 690 BC until 664 BC.

Nubians played a major role in Egyptian civilization, both at its beginning and near its end. Nubia is an ancient Black country now located within southern Egypt and northern Sudan. Dr. Bruce Williams from the University of Chicago published in 1979, after extensive archaeological investigation, that a great Black Nubian dynasty preceded the 1st Egyptian dynasty by several hundred years and introduced all of the principles of civilization, which were later brought to fruition by the ancient Egyptians. Evidence of an advanced political organization with Pharaohs, an advanced writing system with hieroglyphics, and an advanced religious concept with Horus and Osiris were all found to precede the first Egyptian dynasty.

During the Ninth Century BC, Egypt became dominated by foreign rulers, including the Libyans and Assyrians, and again looked for help from her southern Black neighbor. The Nubian Emperor Piankhy conquered all of Egypt and became the first ruler of the 25th Egyptian dynasty. He sponsored a cultural revival in Egypt and resurrected the linguistic and artistic style of the old and middle Egyptian kingdoms. He refurbished all the Egyptian temples and monuments and had many new pyramids and other buildings erected.

It was during this 25th Egyptian dynasty, between 800 BC and 654 BC, called the "Nubian Renaissance," that Africans were also responsible for tremendously influencing the first American civilization called the Olmec civilization. Speculation

Stone Heads from Mexico

as to a possible African element in the first major American civilization began in 1858 AD, when the first of many colossal stone heads were discovered by Mexican peasants. These colossal heads were over eight feet in height and weighed over 10 tons each. The colossal heads were carbon dated to 800 BC and all have typical Nubian features including full lips, fleshy noses, and Africoid facial contours. The ancient Egyptian harbor at Tanis is the only other place in the world with colossal stone heads of ancient Nubian Blacks.

Olmec Colossal Stone Head

Dr. Ivan Van Sertima studied extensively the Egypto-Nubian presence in ancient Mexico and found tremendous technological and cultural contributions made to the Olmec civilization by Nubians.

These technological advancements included the art of mummification, the art of pyramid building, and the skills needed to transport massive blocks of stone for long distances. Buildings required great mathematical precision in the laying, reveling, and fitting of the stone, and this was done for the first time in ancient America with Nubian instructors. Dr. Barry Fell of Harvard says the Egypto-Nubian hieroglyphic writing system has been found as far north as eastern Canada, among the Micmac tribe after spreading from its Olmec center. Bronze technology was also given to the Olmecs in addition to the Egyptian calendar.

Cultural traits adopted by the Olmecs from the Egypto-Nubians included the use of the color purple, the artificial beard, and the double crown headdress for signifying royalty. Professor Wiercinski, a Polish skull and skeletal expert, says that 13.5% of the bones found in one Olmec cemetery were African, and that many were dressed in a royal or priest fashion and were lying side by side with a native American female.

During the Nubian renaissance, long before Christopher Columbus and even before Jesus Christ, Blacks were masters of the old world of Egypt and the new world of America. Dr. Van Sertima says that this fact in itself opens a new historical window from which to view the history of America and of the entire Black race.

REFERENCES AND ADDITIONAL READING

De Roo, P. (1900) <u>History of America Before Columbus</u>. Philadelphia: J.P. Lippincott.

Hyman, M. (1994) Black<u>s Before America.</u> Trenton, NJ: Africa World Press.

Irwin, C. (1963) <u>Fair Gods, and Stone Faces</u>. New York: St. Martin's Press.

Jairazbhoy, R.A. (1992) <u>Rameses III: Father of Early America</u>. Chicago: Frontline International.

Jairazbhoy, R.A. (1974) <u>Ancient Egyptians and Chinese in America.</u> New Jersey: Rowman and Littlefield.

Nettleford, R. & Hyatt, V. (eds.) (1995) <u>Race, Discourse and Origin of the Americas.</u> Washington, DC: Smithsonian Institute Press.

Peterson, F. (1959) <u>Ancient Mexico</u>. New York: Putnam and Sons.

Van Sertima, I. (ed.) (1992) <u>African Presence in Early America.</u> New Brunswick, New Jersey: Transaction Publishers.

Van Sertima, I. (ed.) (1998) <u>Early America Revisited.</u> New Brunswick, New Jersey: Transaction Publishers.

Van Sertima, I. (1977)<u> They Came Before Columbus.</u> New York: Random House.

Von Wuthenau, A. (1975) <u>Unexpected Faces in Ancient America.</u> New York: Crown Publishers.

Von Wuthennau, A. (1969) T<u>he Art of Terracotta Pottery in Pre-Columbian South and Central America.</u> New York: Crown.

Wiener, L. (1922) <u>Africa and the Discovery of America</u>. Philadelphia: Innes and Sons.

BLACK MULTI-GENIUSES

World history has produced many men who have been described as geniuses but very few have ever been described as multi-genius. European historians have used the term multi-genius to describe such men as Aristotle and Leonardo de Vinci. However, these historians have never described a Black person as a multi-genius despite the fact that there have been just as many Black multi-geniuses as there are White. In fact, the world's first and greatest multi-genius in recorded history is a small Black Egyptian named Imhotep. Others include Benjamin Banneker and Cheikh Anta Diop.

Cheikh Anta Diop was born in 1923 in Western Senegal. He completed his bachelor's degree in Senegal and his doctorate degree in Paris. Diop began as an extremely promising physicist who performed experiments in the world famous laboratory of Marie Curie (who earlier had won the Nobel Prize for the discovery of radiation). At a time when only a handful of people in the world understood Einstein's Theory of Relativity, Diop translated the theory into his native Senegalese language of Wolof.

In midstream, Diop decided to change his Ph.D. dissertation to ancient Egyptian history and to use his scientific background to prove that ancient Egyptians were Black skinned indigenous Africans, who taught the Greeks what later became Western civilization. Diop wanted Black people around the world to be able to claim the ancient Egyptians with great pride as their ancestors.

Diop's Ph.D. dissertation was rejected three times until he developed a chemical process for testing melanin in the skin of Egyptian mummies and proved that ancient Egyptians were a dark skinned race. He also became an expert in linguistics and proved that the Egyptian language was African and that it was genetically related to a family of African languages, including his own native Wolof. In 1966, Diop built a radiocarbon laboratory in Senegal for carbon-14 dating to help prove that the human race first started in Africa.

CHEIKH ANTA DIOP

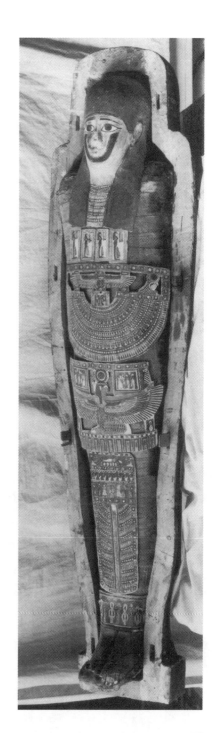

DIOP TOOK SKIN
FROM AN EGYPTIAN
MUMMY AND PROVED
IT HAD LARGE
AMOUNTS OF
MELANIN.

Another Black genius was Benjamin Banneker, who was born near Baltimore, Maryland in 1732. At the age of 22, he looked at a pocket watch from England and constructed America's first large wooden clock in his front yard, which kept accurate time for over 20 years. White people traveled from five neighboring states to see this unusual clock built by a Black man.

The first scientific book ever written by an African American is believed to be the astronomical <u>Almanac</u>. It was first published by Banneker in 1792, and accurately predicted eclipses, high and low tides, positions of the planets, times for sunrise and sunset, and many other useful items. Banneker was also the most important member of a federal surveying team, that laid out plans for the construction of Washington, D.C.

The first and greatest of all multi-geniuses was Imhotep, who served the Egyptian Pharaoh Zoser around 2980 BC. His titles included Chief Physician, Grand Vizier, Chief Architect, Head Priest, Chief Scribe, and Astronomer. Imhotep was the real "Father of Medicine", and his reputation as a healer was so great that he was worshiped as the "God of Medicine" by Persians, Greeks, and Romans over a period of 3,000 years.

As Grand Vizier, Imhotep served as the King's supervisor of all departments of State including: the judiciary, the treasury, the Army and Navy, agriculture, and on all of the king's construction projects. Imhotep's father was a distinguished architect who taught his son very well. Imhotep built the first and largest stone structure in recorded history called the Step Pyramid of Zakkarah. It was designed to become the tomb of Pharaoh Zoser and consisted of large blocks of limestone, that reached 195 feet high and 396 feet wide at the base.

As Chief Priest, Imhotep was responsible for reading religious text during burial ceremonies. Common people held the Chief Priest in high esteem because they believed that he influenced the final destinies of dead spirits and also served as a mediator between the king and unseen powers of the universe.

AT 22, USING A BORROWED WATCH AS A MODEL, A POCKET KNIFE AS HIS ONLY TOOL, HE CONSTRUCTED THE FIRST CLOCK MADE IN AMERICA.—IT KEPT ACCURATE TIME FOR OVER 20 YEARS!

BENJAMIN BANNEKER
ASTRONOMER—CITY PLANNER

ON THE ADVICE OF THOMAS JEFFERSON, HE WAS PLACED ON THE COMMISSION WHICH SURVEYED AND LAID OUT THE CITY OF WASHINGTON, D.C.!

PLANNING FOR PEACE IN TIME OF WAR WAS ADVOCATED BY BANNEKER IN HIS FAMOUS ALMANAC IN 1793!

Surgical instruments of Imhotep

Imhotep Father of Medicine

Step Pyramid, The World's First Stone Structure

Imhotep was such a great philosopher that much of his advice has been passed along for 5000 years, such as, "Eat, drink, and be merry for tomorrow we die." As an astronomer, Imhotep believed that heavenly bodies exerted a profound influence on the welfare of men, so he carefully charted the movements of the planets, the moon, the sun, the eclipses, and the stars.

Malcolm X once wrote that history is best prepared to reward all research. With just a little research, one could uncover the enormous contributions for the benefit and betterment of mankind made by our brilliant Black multi-geniuses.

REFERENCES AND ADDITIONAL READING

Adams, R. (1969) <u>Great Negroes: Past and Present</u>. Chicago: Afro-Am Publishing Co.

Diop, C.A. (1978) <u>The Cultural Unity of Black Africa.</u> Chicago: Third World Press.

Diop, C.A. (1981) <u>The African Origin of Civilization: Myth or Reality</u>. Westport Connecticut: Lawrence Hill and Co.

Diop, C.A. (1981) "The Origin of the Ancient Egyptians" in Mokhtar, G. (ed.) <u>General History of Africa</u>. Berkeley: University of California Press.

Diop, C.A. (1991) <u>Civilization or Barbarism.</u> Westport Connecticut: Lawrence Hill and Co.

Finch, C. (1990) <u>The African Background to Medical Science</u>. London, UK: Billing and Sons Ltd, Worcester.

Hayden, R. (1992) <u>7 African-American Scientists</u>. Frederick, Maryland: Twenty-First Century Books.

Hurry, J. (1987) <u>Imhotep: The Egyptian God of Medicine</u>. Chicago: Ares Publishers Inc.

Rogers, J.A. (1989) <u>Africa's Gift to America.</u> St. Petersburg, Florida: Helga Rogers Publishing.

Rogers, J.A. (1946) <u>World's Great Men of Color</u>. New York: Collier Books.

Sally, C. (1993) <u>The Black 100</u>. New York: Carol Publishing Group.

Stetter, C. (1993) <u>The Secret Medicine of the Pharaohs</u>. Carol Streams, Illinois: Quintessence Publishing Co. Inc.

Van Sertima, I. (ed.) (1991) <u>Blacks in Science</u>. New Brunswick. New Jersey: Transaction Publishers.

Van Sertima, I. (ed.) (1986) <u>Great African Thinkers.</u> New Brunswick, New Jersey: Transaction Publishers.

HANNIBAL: AFRICAN MILITARY GENIUS

Hannibal Barca (247-183 BC) from the ancient city of Carthage (North Africa), is considered the greatest military genius of all time. The maneuvers and strategies this Black general used to defeat the larger Roman armies repeatedly over a period of 14 years while on Italian soil have been studied for centuries at military academies throughout the world. Moreover, it is believed that the German army successfully used several of Hannibal's strategies in World War I, including the "Schlieffen Plan" of envelopment that was based on Hannibal's famous battle at Cannae.

Ancient Carthage was a magnificent city founded on the Northern coast of Africa (near present day Tunisia) around 800 BC. This city was the undisputed leader in maritime trade and commerce throughout the Mediterranean Sea and most of the known world for over 400 years. During the third century before Christ, Rome became powerful enough to challenge its African rival, and eventually they fought three bloody wars called the Punic Wars. Hannibal's father was also a great general named Hamilcar Barca, who lost to Rome in the first Punic War that was fought for control of the Mediterranean Sea and trade with several neighboring islands, especially Sicily.

After losing the first Punic War (264-241 BC), Hamilcar Barca conquered most of Southern Spain (called Iberia by the Romans) in an attempt to replace or compensate for the trade and commerce lost to Rome. It is believed that Barcelona, Spain was named for the Barca family. Hannibal's father made his sons pledge undying hatred for Rome and eventual revenge for Carthaginian losses during the first Punic War. Hamilcar also made certain his sons were trained in the finest African military tradition, and also had them tutored by superlative Greek scholars. Hannibal was the eldest and most brilliant of the sons and could speak five languages, including Greek and Latin, before age 20.

Upon the death of his father, Hannibal was appointed supreme commander of the Carthaginian military at the tender age of 25. After Rome continued to attack Carthaginian allies and suppress trade routes, Hannibal decided to organize the world's most diversified army and attack Rome. His 90,000 men included soldiers from several different North African tribes, in addition to swarthy Spaniards, and white Celts and Gauls. His multiracial army was also multilingual and required over a dozen interpreters for Hannibal's every word. Few military minds today would have given Hannibal much of a chance against a powerful homogeneous single race, single language Roman army fighting in defense of its own homeland.

Hannibal's other greatest challenge was getting his army into Italy since Rome controlled the waterways. His decision to march his massive army over the Alps had never been attempted before and is again a testimony to his great genius. For example, in crossing turbid rivers, such as the Rhone, Hannibal would build large flat rafts and cover them with dirt so as to trick the elephants on board. The larger elephants were forced to cross upstream, which provided a partial damming of the river, that allowed the smaller pack animals and horses to cross down stream.

On one occasion, large 1,000-ton boulders blocked Hannibal's only path, and his soldiers were afraid they would have to turn back. Hannibal drew upon the Greek science he had learned and ordered his men to cut down all the neighboring trees and place them under the boulders. Once the trees were set afire and the boulders became so hot they glowed, he then ordered his men to pour large amounts of vinegar on the stones, which caused the boulders to breakup into smaller movable pieces.

Hannibal repeatedly provided ingenious solutions to apparently unsolvable problems that made this African appear god-like in the eyes of his soldiers. However, traveling over 1000 miles and five months through the Pyrenees Mountains and the Alps was still very treacherous, and Hannibal lost half his army through harsh weather exposure and battling with hostile tribes seeking plunder.

Once Hannibal reached Northern Italy, he attempted to enlarge his army by telling local inhabitants that he had come to liberate them from the oppressive Romans. He had the wisdom to form an alliance with several of the larger tribes by using his army to defeat their local

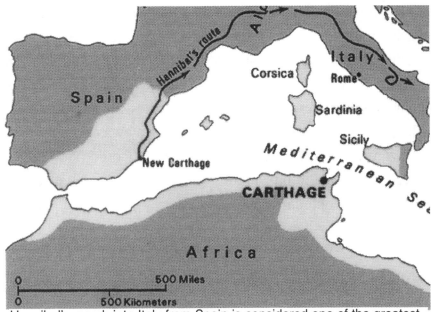

Hannibal's march into Italy from Spain is considered one of the greatest feats in military history.

enemies. Hannibal thoroughly interviewed all the local leaders and also sent out scouts to determine the best areas for battle and ambush. He would also thoroughly investigate the character of his opposing Roman generals to determine which generals were most likely to be short tempered, impetuous, and prone to mistakes. The Roman Republic elected two different generals every six months and allowed those generals to rotate leadership every other day. Hannibal only did battle when the general he considered less capable was in charge.

In his first battle against the Roman army (217 BC) at the Trebia River, Hannibal hid several thousand of his best soldiers and cavalry in the swampy river bed overnight. Once the Romans marched past the hidden troops, Hannibal's army was able to attack them from the front and rear and destroyed them easily. The Romans soon regrouped and sent a second army after the Carthaginians. Hannibal studied a local lake adjacent to a steep mountain cliff (Lake Trasimene) and chose

Coins from Carthage with Hannibal on one side and His elephant on the other.

this as his second battleground. He noted that the lake produced a heavy fog in the morning, which allowed his soldiers to hide in the cliffs and pounce upon the unsuspecting Roman army, which could not see his troops until it was too late.

After having two large armies slaughtered by Hannibal in ambush, the Roman Senate decided to canvas all of Southern Italy and to produce the largest army in their history, which would only fight Hannibal in open combat. Over 80,000 troops were recruited to fight against Hannibal who had less than 40,000 soldiers left in his multiracial army. Hannibal defeated the large Roman army in a strategy that was copied for centuries thereafter. Noting that the Romans fought only in rigid columns, he placed his poorest Gaullic soldiers in a large semicircle facing the Romans and his best African soldiers far to the left and right of this semicircle. As the rigid Roman columns beat back the semicircle of Gaullic infantry, which went from convex to concave, they failed to notice that Hannibal's best African soldiers were forming a vice on the left and right. Hannibal's crack Numidian cavalry fought their way to the rear of the Roman army, which was now surrounded. In this deadly Battle of Cannae, more than 70,000 Roman soldiers were killed within three hours, which in comparison was more that one third of all Americans killed during the four years of World War II.

One of the greatest mysteries of all time is why Hannibal did not attack the city of Rome after destroying its entire army. Many of his officers were bitterly disappointed. Some historians suggest that Hannibal may have become compassionate after seeing 70,000 Romans dead on the battlefield. Perhaps he felt he could not penetrate the fortified walls without battering rams and other wall storming equipment he did not have. Over the next 14 years, Hannibal conquered all of Southern Italy virtually unopposed since Roman armies were afraid to confront him. Hannibal divided his war spoils and booty between his troops and Carthage, which disposed both to hold him in high esteem.

After many years, a brilliant young Roman general named Publius Cornelius Scipio, who spent most of his life studying Hannibal's warfare techniques, convinced the Roman Senate that Hannibal would leave Italy if Rome attacked Carthage. Scipio was also able to turn almost all of Hannibal's North African allies against him including the powerful Numidians by making outlandish and unfulfilled promises of land and riches. Upon returning to Africa (202 BC), Hannibal could not defeat the combined alliance of Africans and Romans at the Battle of Zama, and Carthage was forced to surrender. Unable to escape, Hannibal subsequently chose poisoning over imprisonment.

One has to speculate what type of world we would have if Hannibal had destroyed the city of Rome after completely destroying her entire army. Perhaps the Black Africans of Carthage could have provided a "kinder and gentler" world than the Roman Empire did over the next 700 years.

REFERENCES AND ADDITIONAL READING

Arnold, T. (1886) <u>The Second Punic War</u>. London: Macmillan and Co.

Baker, G. (1929) <u>Hannibal.</u> New York: Dodd Meade.

Cottrell, L. (1988) <u>Hannibal: Enemy of Rome.</u> New York: Da Capo Press, Inc.

De Beer, G. (1959) <u>Alps and Elephants</u>: Hannibal's March. New York: Dutton.

DeGraft-Johnson, J.C. (1954) <u>African Glory</u>. Baltimore: Black Classic Press.

Gilbert, C. (1968) <u>Life and Death of Carthage.</u> New York: Tapinger.

Hyman, M. (1994) <u>Blacks Before America</u>. Trenton, N.J.: Africa World Press.

Jackson, J.G. (1970) <u>Introduction to African Civilizations</u>. New York: Carol Publishing Group.

Lamb, H. (1958) <u>Hannibal: One Man Against Rome</u>. New York: Doubleday.

Law, W. (1866) <u>The Alps of Hannibal</u>. London: Macmillan and Co.

Liddell, H. (1926) <u>Greater than Napoleon - Scipio Africanus</u>. London: William Blackwood and Sons.

Rogers, J.A. (1946) <u>World's Great Men of Color.</u> New York: Collier Books.

Van Sertima, I. (ed.) (1986) <u>Great African Thinkers.</u> New Brunswick, New Jersey: Transaction Publishers.

WHO ARE THE DOGON?

An illiterate West African tribe known as the Dogon, who live in the Bandiagara Cliffs of Southeastern Mali, startled the scientific world in the 1950s when it was

Dogon Dancers with bird mask

discovered that their priests have had extremely complex knowledge of astronomy for at least 700 years. They have known for centuries about the rings of Saturn, the moons of Jupiter, the spiral structure of the Milky Way Galaxy, and intricate details about the stars, including their mass and orbits. Much of the complex astrological knowledge that the Dogon have had since the 13th century either cannot be confirmed by modern scientists or was not discovered until the 20th century. Kenneth Brecher of the Massachusetts Institute of Technology was dumfounded and stated bluntly: "The Dogon have no business knowing any of this." Robert Temple, an acclaimed member of the Royal Astronomical Society, speculates in his book The Sirius Mystery that "space-beings from the Sirius star-system must have brought this marvelous knowledge down to the Africans."

Two French Anthropologists, Marcel Griaule and Germaine Dieterlen, lived and worked with the Dogon from 1931 to 1956, and eventually became so loved and trusted that they were initiated into the tribe. After 16 years of stage by stage initiations, the Dogon called a conference and revealed to these Europeans their intimate secret knowledge of the solar system that was eventually recorded in a book entitled <u>The Pale Fox</u>. The Frenchmen were told that our solar system consists of a fixed star with planets rotating around this star and moons rotating around the planets. They said a force we describe as "gravity" was responsible for holding the planets and moons in place. The Dogon gave names and a complete description of

Dogon Mask

the properties and behavior of the planets, moons, and fixed stars such as Polaris, Sirius, and the Pleiades. Mars, for example, was called "Yapunu toll" meaning "planet of menstruation" perhaps because of its red color. A calendar based on the six positions or phases of Venus determined when the Dogon would plant and harvest their food for best results. However, no aspect of Dogon knowledge has created more astonishment than their description of the properties of the star known as Sirius B ("po tolo" to the Dogon). It is incomprehensible to modern scientists how the Dogon could

know so much about Sirius B, an invisible star to the naked eye, located 51 trillion miles away. The Frenchmen were told that Sirius B is the sky's tiniest and yet heaviest star and has a 50 year elliptical orbit around Sirius A, the brightest star in the sky. The Dogon said that this dwarf star (Sirius B) is the most important star and the origin of all other stars, and that it is composed of a metal heavier and brighter than iron. Although Sirius B is invisible to the naked eye, the Dogon have chosen a new astronomer-priest every 60 years when the orbits of Sirius B, Jupiter, and Saturn come into synchronization.

A ceremony called the "sigui" is held and a mask is carved to celebrate this 60-year event. Griaule and Dieterlen said they were shown a cave in Ibi, Mali, that contained 12 sigui ceremonial masks, which would date the ceremonies back to the 13th century. The first Western report of Sirius B was not until 1862 by Alvan Clark who observed the companion star through his new telescope. The Dogon told of several other companion stars around Sirius A that were not confirmed by modern astrophysicists until 1979, with the "Einstein" orbiting observatory. The Dogon also have an annual "bado" celebration that honors the one year period in which Sirius B rotates on its own axis. Modern scientists still can not confirm this one-year rotation on its own axis.

Charles Finch, in his book entitled <u>The Star of Deep Beginnings</u> says that the Dogon have never been proven wrong in any of their descriptions of the properties and behavior of Sirius B, and that they are also probably correct in calling Sirius B the mother of all stars. Finch says that Sirius B is as old as the universe (12 billion years) and the closest star to our solar system. Moreover, he states "since all newborn stars (like our sun) are created from older stars, our solar system including Earth and everything in it may owe its very existence to Sirius B as the Dogon say."

The advanced scientific knowledge of the Dogon makes them the most astonishing and enigmatic people in all Africa. Hunter Adams, III of the Argonne National Laboratory admits that in certain domains of astronomy and cosmology the Dogon have no historical peers. He says there is nothing remotely similar to the knowledge of the Dogon in the literature of the ancient Egyptians, Sumerians, Greeks, Chinese, or Medieval Arabs. It is truly a shame that entrenched Western racist attitudes towards African scientific knowledge can only attribute Dogon knowledge to the presence of space aliens. Unfortunately, most agree with Robert Temple of the Royal Astronomical Society of Great Britain that "space-beings from the Sirius star-system must have brought this marvelous knowledge down to the Africans."

REFERENCES AND ADDITIONAL READING

Charroux, R. (1972) <u>The Mysterious Unknown</u>. London: Neville Spearman.

Finch, C. (1998) <u>The Star of Deep Beginnings</u>. Decatur, Georgia: Khenti, Inc.

Ford, D. (1954) <u>African Worlds</u>. Oxford: Oxford University Press.

Griaule, M. & Dieterlen, G. (1986) <u>The Pale Fox.</u> Chino Valley, Arizona: Continuum Foundation.

Hawking, S. (1990) <u>A Brief History of Time.</u> New York: Bantam Books.

Michanowsky, G. (1977) <u>The Once and Future Star</u>. New York: Hawthorn.

Rawlinson, G. (1885) <u>The Seven Great Monarchies of the Ancient Eastern World.</u> New York: John B. Alden.

Smoot, G. & Davidson, K. (1993) <u>Wrinkles in Time</u>. New York: Avon Books.

Temple, R. (1976) <u>The Sirius Mystery</u>. New York: St. Martins Press, Inc.

Tompkins, P. (1978) <u>Secrets of the Great Pyramid</u>. New York: Harper Colophon Edition.

Van Sertima, I. (ed.) (1991) <u>Blacks in Science</u>. New Brunswick, New Jersey: Transaction Books.

Wolf, F. (1988) <u>Parallel Universes.</u> New York: Simon and Shuster.

GREAT AFRICAN CIVILIZATIONS

The conquering nations throughout history have always rewritten, or destroyed, the history of the nations they conquer. Racism and the brutal and devastating effects of slavery only intensified the need to change African history. It was argued that Africans were pagans, savages, and heathens in need of salvation and that the best thing the slave traders did for Black people was to have dragged our ancestors to the Americas in chains, because they lacked the intellectual capacity to succeed. Nothing could be further from the truth! While the Moors were re-civilizing Europe, great empires were thriving in Western Africa and frequently traded with the Moors. These included the empires of Ghana, Mali, and Songhay, which prospered between 700 AD and 1600 AD.

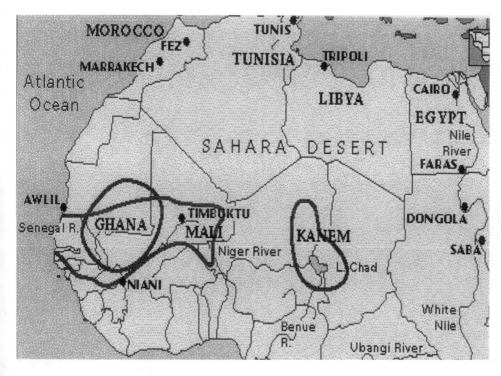

The Mali Empire replaced the Ghana Empire as the most powerful state in Western Africa until the Songhay Empire replaced it.

The founders of Ghana were known as the Soninkes, and they were experts in making tools and weapons with iron. In fact, their iron weapons helped them to conquer the neighboring tribes and to form their empire. They are also said to have had an inexhaustible supply of gold. It was so plentiful that the emperor passed a law, which said that all gold in nugget form belonged to him and that the people could only use gold dust. It was said that without this precaution, gold would have become so plentiful that it would have lost its value. One gold nugget was so large that it was used as a hitching post for the ruler's favorite horse. Ghana was also famous as a trading center where locally produced metal tools, jewelry, leather, and cotton clothes were traded for imports from Moorish Spain and Morocco.

The Sankore Mosque in Timbuktu became an important Islamic house of worship.

The Mali Empire began in 1230 AD with King Sundiata. He gained control of all the trade that had been monopolized by Ghana. In 1342, Mansa Musa made a pilgrimage to Mecca, which made the Mali Empire world famous. He took a caravan of 60,000 people to Mecca and gave away so much gold as presents that the gold market in the world was devalued for 12 years. When he was asked in Cairo how he became emperor, he said that his brother, Emperor Abubakari II took 2,000 ships in 1311 AD, sailed west, and never returned. Ivan Van Sertima in his book They Came Before Columbus, acknowledges Abubakari II as one of the discovers of America who preceded Columbus. The Mali Empire had a standing army of 100,000 men and is said to have included an area the size of Western Europe.

The Songhay Empire rose to supremacy approximately 1457 AD and eventually became as large as the United States of America. The Songhay Empire was also a prosperous trading center but became world famous as a center of advanced culture and higher education. Famous universities were established in the cities of Gao, Jenne, and Timbuktu, which employed thousands of teachers who offered courses that included astronomy, mathematics, medicine, hygiene, music, and many others. Jenne also had a medical school that was especially famous for training surgeons in difficult operations such as cataract surgery. Professor Ahmed Baba, who was chancellor of the University of Sankore in Timbuktu, was the author of more than 40 books and had a personal library of 1,600 volumes; which he said was small, compared to the library of his colleagues. During the slave trade, many of the slaves from the former Songhay Empire were highly educated and were credited with teaching Caribbean and American farmers successful agricultural techniques. They also invented various tools and equipment to lessen the burden of their daily work. The Songhay Empire prospered until 1591 when it was finally conquered by Moorish invaders from North Africa.

REFERENCES AND ADDITIONAL READING

Brooks, L. (1971) <u>African Achievements</u>. Stamford, CT: De Gustibus Press.

Chu,D. & Skinner, E. (1990) <u>A Glorious Age in Africa: The Story of Three Great African Empires.</u> Trenton, New Jersey.

Davidson, B. (1965) <u>A History of West Africa</u>. Garden City, NJ: Doubleday.

Davidson, B. (1964) <u>The African Past</u>. Boston: Little-Brown.

Davidson, B. (1959) <u>The Lost Cities of Africa.</u> Boston: Little-Brown.

DeGraft-Johnson, J.C. (1954) <u>African Glory</u>. Baltimore: Black Classic Press.

Dobbler, L. & Brown, W. (1965) <u>Great Rulers of the African Past.</u> New York: Doubleday.

Drachler, J. <u>African Heritage</u>. New York: Collier Books.

Hyman, M. (1994) <u>Blacks Before America</u>. Trenton, NJ: Africa World Press.

Jackson, J. (1990) <u>Introduction to African Civilization.</u> New York: Carol Publishing Group.

Motley, M. (1969) <u>Africa: Its Empires, Nations, and People</u>. Detroit: Wayne State University Press.

Robinson, C., Battle, R., & Robinson, E. (1987) <u>The Journey of the Songhai People.</u> Philadelphia: Farmer Press.

Rogers, J.A. (1972) <u>World's Great Men of Color.</u> New York: Macmillian Publishing Co.

Williams, C. (1987) <u>The Destruction of Black Civilization</u>. Chicago: Third World Press.

THE MOORS

During the European Dark Ages, between the 7th and 14th centuries AD, the Moorish Empire in Spain became one of the world's finest civilizations. General Tarik, and his Black Moorish army from Morocco, conquered Spain after a week long battle with King Roderick in 711 AD. (The word tariff and the Rock of Gibraltar were named after him). They found that Europe, with the assistance of the Catholic Church, had returned almost to complete barbarism. The population was 90% illiterate and had lost all of the civilizing principles that were passed on by the ancient Greeks and Romans.

"The Moorish Chief" by Eduard Charlemont

The Moors reintroduced mathematics, medicine, agriculture, and the physical sciences. The clumsy Roman numerals were replaced by Arabic figures including the zero and the decimal point. As Dr. Van Sertima says, "You can't do higher mathematics with Roman numerals." The Moors introduced agriculture to Europe including cotton, rice, sugar cane, dates, ginger, lemons, and strawberries. They also taught them how to store grain for up to 100 years and build underground grain silos. They established a world famous silk industry in Spain. The Moorish achievement in hydraulic engineering was outstanding. They constructed an aqueduct, that conveyed water through lead pipes from the mountains to the city. They taught them how to mine for minerals on a large scale, including copper, gold, silver, tin, lead, and aluminum. Spain soon became the world center for high quality sword blades and shields. Spain was eventually manufacturing up to 12,000 blades and shields per year. Spanish craft and woolen became world famous. The Moorish craftsman also produced world class glass, pottery, vases, mosaics, and jewelry.

The Moors introduced to Europe paved, lighted streets with raised sidewalks for pedestrians, flanked by uninterrupted rows of buildings. Paved and lighted streets did not appear in London or Paris for hundreds of years. They constructed thousands of public markets and mills in each city; Cordova alone had 5,000 of each. They also introduced to Spain underwear and bathing with soap. Their public baths numbered in the thousands when bathing in the rest of Europe was frowned upon as a diabolical custom to be avoided by all good Christians. Poor hygiene contributed to the plagues in the rest of Europe. Moorish monarchs dwelled in sumptuous palaces while the crowned heads of England, France, and Germany lived in barns, that lacked windows, toilets, and chimneys, and with only a hole in the roof as the exit for smoke. Human waste material was thrown in the streets since no bathrooms were present.

Education was made mandatory by the Moors, while 90% of Europe was illiterate, including the kings and queens. The Moors introduced public libraries to Europe with 600,000 books housed in Cordova alone. They established 17 outstanding universities in Spain. Since Africa is a matriarchal society, women were also encouraged to devote themselves to serious study, and it was only in Spain that one could find female doctors, lawyers, and scientists.

Moorish schoolteachers knew that the world was round and taught geography from a globe. They produced expert maps with all sea and land routes accurately located with respect to latitude and longitude; while also introducing compasses to Europe. They were such expert shipbuilders that they were able to use their geography expertise to import and export as far away as India and China. It was not by accident that a Moor named Pietro Olonzo Nino was the chief navigator for Christopher Columbus on the flagship Santa Maria. He is said to have argued with Columbus as to who really discovered America. One of the worst mistakes the Moors made was to introduce gunpowder technology from China into Europe, because their enemies adopted this weapon and used it to drive them out of Spain. Europe then took the 700 years of civilization and education re-taught to them by the Moors and used this knowledge to attack Africa.

While the Moors were re-civilizing Europe, great empires were thriving in Western Africa and frequently traded with the Moors. These included the empires of Ghana, Mali, and Songhay, which prospered between 700 AD and 1600 AD. Africa was not a dark continent awaiting European civilization. In fact, Black African Egyptians and Black African Moors are credited with civilizing Europe.

REFERENCES AND ADDITIONAL READING

Bennett, N. (1975) <u>Africa and Europe.</u> New York: Africana Publishing Co.

Bovill, E. (1970) <u>The Golden Trade of the Moors.</u> London: Oxford University Press.

Davidson, B. (1971) <u>Discovering Our African Heritage</u>. Boston: Ginn & Co.

DeGraft-Johnson, J.C. (1954) <u>African Glory</u>. Baltimore: Black Classic Press.

Jackson, J. (1990) <u>Introduction to African Civilization</u>. New York: Carol Publishing Group.

Lane-Poole, S. (1990) <u>The Story of the Moors in Spain</u>. Baltimore: Black Classic Press.

Rogers, J.A. (1968) <u>Sex and Race</u>. St. Petersburg, FL: Helga Rogers Publishing.

Rogers, J.A. (1972) <u>World's Great Men of Color.</u> New York: Macmillan Publishing Co.

Scobie, E. (1962) <u>Africa in Portugal.</u> London: Flamingo.

Scobie, E. (1994) <u>Global Afrikan Presence.</u> New York: A & B Books Publishers.

Scott, S. (1904) <u>History of the Moorish Empire in Europe.</u> J.P. Lippincott.

Van Sertima, I. (ed.) (1991) <u>The Moorish Conquest of Europe</u>. New Brunswick, New Jersey: Transaction Books.

Williams, C. (1976) <u>The Destruction of Black Civilization</u>. Chicago: Third World Press.

Windsor, R. (1969) <u>From Babylon to Timbuktu.</u> New York: Exposition Press.

Woodson, C. (1939) <u>African Heroes and Heroines</u>. Washington DC: Associated Publishers.

BLACK POPES

The Crucifixion of Jesus viewed from an Alabama cotton plantation

Black Roman Africans made significant contributions to the growth of Christianity and the development of the Roman Catholic faith. The three greatest scholars and founding theologians of Christianity were all Roman Africans including Tetulian, Cyperian, and St. Augustine. However, the greatest contribution was probably made by the three Black popes who were Pope Victor I, Pope Miltiades, and Pope Galasius I.

Pope Victor I was the 14th pope and served from 189 AD - 199 AD. In 189 AD, the date of Easter was a matter of great controversy. In Asia, Easter was celebrated on the 14th day after the full moon, which meant that some Christians were celebrating lent while others were celebrating resurrection. Pope Victor I declared that Easter would only be celebrated on Sunday and that he would excommunicate all of the Christians of Asia if they failed to abide by his ruling. Easter has been on Sunday ever since. Under the influence of the Black theologian Tetulian, the Black Pope Victor I also declared that Latin would replace Greek as the official language of the Roman church. Both Victor and Tetulian only wrote in Latin thereafter. Pope Victor I is now celebrated as a saint with a feast day of July 28th.

At the same time that Black Romans controlled the world religiously with Victor and Tetullian, the Black Romans gained control of the world politically and militarily in 193 AD, when the Black Roman African Septimius Severus became the Roman Emperor. He remembered his roots by making large donations to the urban poor and employing them in extensive building campaigns. The month of September was named after Septimius Severus who was seceded as emperor of the Roman Empire by his Black son Caracalla from 211 AD until 217 AD.

The second Black pope was Pope Miltiades who served from 311 AD until 314 AD as the 32nd pope. All Christians were persecuted when Miltiades took office until he obtained an edict of toleration signed by Emperor Galerius, which put an end to the great persecutions and allowed the Christians to come out of their catacombs. Pope Miltiades also convinced Emperor Maxentius to return all church buildings and possessions, which had been confiscated during the

Roman coin depicting Jesus with wooly hair.

persecutions. It was also during the reign of Pope Miltiades that the Emperor Constantine was converted to Christianity after he saw the cross in a vision.

Constantine's army marched into Rome in 312 AD and overthrew the tyrant Maxentius. He subsequently made Christianity the official religion of the Roman Empire. Miltiades was made a saint with his feast celebrated on December 10. The Black Roman theologian, St. Augustine, called Pope Miltiades "an excellent pontiff, a true son of peace, and father of Christians."

The third Black pope was Galasius I, our 49th pope, who took office 492 AD (exactly 1,000 years before America was so-called "discovered"). He is described by his contemporaries as "famous all over the world for his learning and holiness." Galasius I was devoted to uplifting the poor and weak and commanded his bishops to donate 25% of their revenue to charity, stressing that "nothing is more becoming to the priestly office than the protection of the poor and the weak."

Pope Galasius I is also credited with ending the pagan ritual of Lupercalia in which young men would dress in skins and strike any woman they met with a whip, which was supposed to confer fertility and to chase away bad luck. He replaced Lupercalia with the "feast of the purification of the blessed virgin" now called "Candlemas". Galasius I is most famous for his firm letter to Emperor Anastasius about the need for independence of church and state. He told the emperor that the world is governed by two great powers: that of the popes and that of kings; but the authority of the popes is so much greater because on judgment day, popes will have to render an account to God for the soul of kings. As were the other two African popes, Galasius I was also made a saint and his feast day is held on November 21.

Contrary to the belief of those who call Christianity a White man's religion, Christianity was founded with the genius of three Black theologians, and further developed and propelled by devoted contributions from three Black Roman African popes.

REFERENCES AND ADDITIONAL READING

Brusher, J. (1959) <u>Popes Through the Ages</u>. Princeton.

Holtzclaw, R. (1980) <u>The Saints Go Marching In.</u> Keeble Press Inc.

Khamit-Kush, I. (1983) <u>What They Never Told You in History Class</u>. Bronx, NY: Luxorr Publications.

Loomis, L.R. (1916) <u>Book of the Popes.</u> New York.

Ottley, R. (1952) <u>No Green Pastures.</u> London: John Murray.

Scobie, E. (1994) <u>Global Afrikan Presence</u>. New York: A & B Books Publishers.

Van Sertima, I. (ed.) (1993) <u>African Presence in Early Europe.</u> New Brunswick, New Jersey: Transaction Publishers.

AFRICAN MEDICINE

Although Africans and people of African descent are seldom given credit in standard textbooks, African wisdom contributed greatly toward the development of modern medicine. For example, in Western Africa during the Songhay Empire, about 1457 AD, (when Europe was still in its "Dark Ages") the city of Jenne had a medical school which employed hundreds of teachers and was world famous for training surgeons in difficult operations such as cataract surgery. They also taught the pharmacological use of over 1000 animal and plant products for the treatment of medical illnesses. Many of these same medicines in pill or liquid form are used today. For example, castor seeds, the source of castor oil, was used for constipation and castor oil is still used today. Kaolin was used for diarrhea and is still used today in kaopectate. Night blindness caused by Vitamin "A" deficiency was treated with Ox liver, which is rich in vitamin "A". Vitamin "C" deficiency was treated with onions, which have a high vitamin "C" content.

The antibiotic penicillin (produced by penicillium mold) and its therapeutic properties were well known by the ancient Egyptians who far exceeded the rest of the ancient world in medical knowledge. However, the presence of the antibiotic tetracycline appears only in the bones of farmers from northern Sudan about 1500 years ago. The ancient Sudanese farmers discovered that streptomyces molds can easily produce tetracycline on stored grain and purposefully used tetracycline to treat infection. There is no evidence that tetracycline antibiotic has been used anywhere else in the world. Tetracycline was not rediscovered until the twentieth century.

More than 40% of modern pharmacological medicines are derived from traditional African medicinal herbs. For example, the Yoruba of Nigeria used the plant Rauwolfia vomitoria as a sedative or tranquilizer to calm agitated or psychotic patients. Modern medicine was able to isolate a substance called reserpine from this plant that was marketed for the same purpose. Reserpine was also discovered to profoundly lower blood pressure and consequently, became one of the first antihypertensive medications.

An Antivacine Society cartoon against cowpox. The British Dr. Edward Jenner only changed the African smallpox inoculation technique by using the less dangerous cowpox germ.

In America, in 1721, an African slave named Onesimus taught his master an age-old African technique for smallpox inoculation in which a pustule from an infected person was ruptured with a thorn and then used to puncture the skin of a non-infected person. Subsequently, during a smallpox epidemic in the Boston, MA area, Dr. Boylston inoculated 241 healthy people by this African technique and only six caught smallpox. During the American Revolutionary War, General George Washington ordered his entire army inoculated against smallpox by this African method. In the 1790's, the British Dr. Edward Jenner only changed the African smallpox inoculation technique by using a less dangerous kind of smallpox germ.

Finally, as recently as 1880 AD in Europe, the mortality rate was almost 100% for mothers delivering their babies by caesarean section (that is, delivering babies through the abdomen). Consequently, the operation was only performed to save the life of the infant. Dr. R. W. Felkin, a missionary, shocked the European medical community when he published in the Edinburgh Medical Journal in 1884, that the Banyoro surgeons in Uganda performed caesarean sections routinely, without harmful effects to the mother or the infant. A group of European surgeons went to study in Uganda for six months before they could successfully learn the advanced surgical techniques demonstrated by the Africans. The Europeans were also taught sophisticated concepts of anesthesia and antisepsis. For example, they were taught to routinely wash the surgeon's hands and the mother's abdomen with alcohol prior to surgery to prevent infection. This antisepsis technique had not been practiced in Europe prior to this African visit.

In summary, Africans have contributed greatly toward the development of modern medicine and deserve to be better acknowledged in our medical textbooks.

REFERENCES AND ADDITIONAL READING

Brothwell, D. & Sandison, A. (eds.) (1967) <u>Disease in Antiquity.</u> Springfield MA: Charles C. Thomas.

Bryant, A. (1966) <u>Zulu Medicine and Medicine-Men.</u> Cape Town: C. Struik.

Finch, C. (1992) <u>Africa and the Birth of Science and Technology</u>. Decatur, GA: Khenti Inc.

Finch, C. (1990) <u>The African Background to Medical Science.</u> London, UK: Billing and Sons Ltd.

Harley, G. (1970) <u>Native African Medicine</u>. London: Frank Cass.

Imperato, P. (1979) <u>African Folk Medicine.</u> Baltimore: York Press.

Johnston, H. (1902) <u>The Uganda Protectorate</u>. London: Hutchison and Co.

Osler, W. (1982) <u>The Evolution of Modern Medicine.</u> Birmingham: The Classics of Medicine Library.

Pankhurst, R. (1990) <u>The Medical History of Ethiopia</u>. Trenton, New Jersey.

Rogers, J. (1991) <u>Africa's Gift to America</u>. St. Petersburg, Florida: Helga Rogers Publishing.

Sofowara, A. (1982) <u>Medicinal Plants and Traditional Medicine in Africa.</u> New York: John Wiley and Sons Limited.

Stetter, C. (1993) <u>The Secret Medicine of the Pharaohs.</u> Trenton, New Jersey: Red Sea Press.

Van Sertima, I. (ed.) (1991) <u>Blacks in Science</u>. New Brunswick, New Jersey: Transaction Books.

Zaslavsky, C. (1973) <u>Africa Counts</u>. Westport: Lawrence Hill & Co.

THE BLACK MADONNA

Isis was a Black African goddess of Nile Valley civilizations whose worship eventually diffused to most of the ancient world. Isis was worshiped by the Nubians well over 300 years before the first Egyptian dynasty. The Egyptians then gave the Isis religion to Greece, Rome, and Western Asia. Gerald Massey says that the religious records of all the world's religions including Hinduism, Buddhism, and Christianity are nothing more than copies of the religious records of the Black goddess Isis, her son Horus, and her husband Osiris. For example, Horus was the first child born from a virgin mother's Immaculate Conception, and he was said to have walked on water just as Jesus later did. The Black goddess Isis is also credited with resurrecting Osiris after he was murdered.

The first "Black Madonna and Child" statues and portraits were of Isis and Horus, and these were taken throughout the world by the Roman Empire. When other religions became more popular, these statues were not destroyed, but simply had their names changed. In India, Isis and Horus became Maya and Buddha in Buddhism or Devaki and Krishna in Hinduism. The Chinese called Isis Kwa-yin, and the Japanese changed the name to Kwannon.

In his 1985 book entitled The Cult of the Black Virgin, Ean Begg was able to identify over 450 images of a Black virgin and child in Europe with over 190 statues in France alone. J.A. Rogers says that Paris was actually named for Isis because Para-Isis means "Place of Isis." He also says that Notre Dame means "Our Lady" and that the cathedral is nothing more than an enlargement of the original Isis temple.

Millions of pilgrims visit the Black Madonna shrines annually because they are believed to possess magical powers, although the statues are now called Mary and Jesus. It is believed that only the Black statues are magical and all pilgrimages stopped whenever the statues were painted white. The Black Madonna's have been credited with healing towns of plagues, bringing dead babies to life, making infertile women pregnant, and saving nations during wars. Many crutches have been left at the feet of the Black Madonnas, who presumably gave their owners the power to walk. One of the most devoted pilgrims of the Black Madonna shrine in Poland is the current Pope John Paul II. He prayed to her image while recovering from his gunshot wound. She is credited with thousands of documented miracles including saving Poland from Russia in 1769. In 1968 alone, the Black Madonna shrine in Poland received over 66,000 thank you letters for healing and other miracles. Pilgrims frequently leave gold watches and rings at the feet of the Black Madonnas in appreciation.

Temple of Isis at Philae, Egypt   Isis & Horus

There are over 450 images of a Black
Madonna and Child in Europe alone.

Church literature absolutely refuses to acknowledge any association of Black Madonnas with Africa. Church officials claim that the Madonnas are Black because of smoke from candles and from dirt and old age. Church officials would never admit that the ancient Egyptians, Greeks, and Romans made pilgrimages until 536 AD to the Isis temple at Philae, Egypt, to seek the same miracles that current pilgrims seek from the Black Madonna shrines. Isis was recognized as a supreme miracle and magic worker and is also credited with teaching mankind the art of curing disease. Isis was able to restore life to the dead as she did with her husband, Osiris, and later with the infant Horus, who was brought back to life after he was killed by a scorpion's sting. Isis was the goddess of corn and grain, water and navigation, and even clothing. She was also called a divine granter of salvation for souls of mankind. The ancient Black Egyptians acknowledged Isis as the source of all their prosperity, including the Nile River.

Isis worship was so strong in Europe that Roman citizens ignored Emperors Augustus and Tuberous, who outlawed Isis worship and persecuted her priests. Emperor Caligulia finally bowed to public pressure and re-established the Isis worship. Emperor Justinian caused an unsuccessful armed insurrection in 536 AD, when he ordered all Isis temples permanently closed.

Religion in general (and the cult of the Black virgin Madonna in specific) is yet another example of the many elements of civilization and civilizing ideas which were brought from Africa into Europe.

REFERENCES AND ADDITIONAL READING

Begg, E. (1985) <u>The Cult of the Black Virgin</u>. New York: Penguin Books.

Budge, E. (1969) <u>The Gods of the Egyptians</u>. New York: Dover.

Doane, T.W. (1882) <u>Bible Myths</u>. New York: Truth Seeker Co.

Grabar, A. (1968) <u>Christian Iconography</u>. Princeton: Princeton University Press.

Jameson, M. (1876) <u>Legends of the Madonna.</u> Boston: Osgood and Co.

MacQuitty, W. (1976) <u>Island of Isis</u>. New York: Charles Scribner's Sons.

Morey, C.R. (1958) <u>Christian Art.</u> New York: Norton.

Rogers, J.A. (1967) <u>Sex and Race</u>. New York: Helga Rogers Publishing.

Patrick, R. (1972) <u>Egyptian Mythology</u>. London: Octopus Books.

Snowden, F. (1970) <u>Blacks in Antiquity.</u> Cambridge: Harvard University Press.

Van Der Merr, F. (1967) <u>Early Christian Art.</u> Chicago: University of Chicago Press.

Van Sertima, I. (ed.) (1984) <u>Black Women in Antiquity</u>. New Brunswick, NJ: Transaction Publishers.

Witt, R. (1971) <u>Isis in the Graeco-Roman World.</u> Ithaca, NY: Cornell.

CHRISTMAS PAGANISM

Ministers encourage their congregations every year, in December, to put Christ back into Christmas. The truth is, Christ never was in Christmas nor will he ever be. The "Christmas Spirit" is created each year by mass media, not to honor Christ, but to sell merchandise. Most merchants obtain more than 50% of their annual revenues at Christmas. Christians in the United States did not practice the heathen custom of exchanging gifts at Christmas until the 19th century, when the merchants revived this Roman custom in order to enrich their coffers.

Michaelangelo's Madonna and Child

Everything about the Christmas holiday is false, corrupt, idolatrous, and pagan. There isn't a shred of truth in Christmas. Mary did not look up to her white, blue eyed husband, Joseph, on December 25th and say "let's call our son's birthday Christmas and celebrate it with a decorated evergreen tree." First of all, the worldwide images of Mary, Joseph, and Jesus were not painted until 1505 AD by Michelangelo and represented his aunt, uncle, and first cousin.

Secondly, every priest knows that Jesus was not born on December 25th. December 25th, as the birth date of Jesus was not adopted until 325 AD, at the Nicaean Council where 318 bishops voted on that as the date. The Eastern Orthodox Church never agreed to this date and continued to celebrate on January 6th. Before 325 AD, most Christians celebrated Christ's birthday on March 25th or September 29th. December 25th was chosen as Christ's birthday because it was the most universally recognized and celebrated holiday in the ancient world. December 25th is the day after the winter solstice, or the first day in winter when the length of daylight begins to increase. Every nation recognized December 25th as the birthday of their sun god including: Mitra, Horus, Hercules, Bacchus, Kristna, Buddha, Adonis, Jupiter, Tammuz, and Saturn.

The Romans called this season "Saturnalia" and celebrated it by exchanging gifts, merriment, revelry, and drunkenness. The sun god Saturn was also the first Santa Claus, which explains why he was omnipresent, that is, could visit every house on Earth in one night; and could know everything about every child's behavior. Santa Claus subsequently became St. Nicholas, a fourth Century bishop of Asia Minor who became the Russian Patron Saint of Children. The St. Nicholas festival was celebrated on December 6th until Queen Victoria moved the date to December 25th and made St. Nicholas the father of Christmas.

Santa Claus did not have a sleigh pulled by reindeer until 1822 when Clement Moore wrote the poem "'Twas the night before Christmas."

The custom of kissing under the mistletoe is believed to have originated with the Celtic midsummer eve ceremony when mistletoe was gathered. During that festival, the men would kiss each other as a display of their homosexuality. The custom was later moved to December and broadened to include both men and women.

The Christmas tree was first decorated by Pagans with small globes or suns to represent the sun god Adonis, who obtained eternal life as an evergreen tree. Gifts were placed under the tree in his honor.

When the Roman Catholic Church could not persuade the public to give up these idolatrous practices, they simply adopted the pagan celebrations and renamed them. Oliver Cromwell and the Puritans had the English parliament ban Christmas from 1642-1662, calling it the "profane man's ranting day." The Pilgrims carried this prohibition to New England. In 1659, Massachusetts passed a law fining anyone caught celebrating Christmas. Public schools remained open on December 25th in Boston until 1870.

It is estimated that Black people spend over $50 billion during the Christmas season and support an economic power system that never worked in their best interest. African Americans would be better served if they abandoned the European pagan holiday of Christmas and used their $50 billion to feed, clothe, house, and educate people toward a better quality of life.

REFERENCES AND ADDITIONAL READING

Anyike, J. (1994) <u>Historical Christianity African Centered.</u> Chicago: Winston-Derek Publishers Group Inc.

Barashango, I. (1983) <u>African People and European Holidays: A Mental Genocide.</u> Silver Spring, MD: Fourth Dynasty Publishing Co.

Ben-Jochannan, Y.A. (1970) <u>African Origins of the Major Western Religions</u>. Baltimore, MD: Black Classic Press.

Churchward, A. <u>The Origin and Evolution of Religion</u>. Kila, MT: Kessinger Publishing Co.

Conzelmann, H. (1973) <u>History of Primitive Christianity</u>. New York: Abingdon Press.

Doane, T.W. (1882) <u>Bible Myths</u>. New York: Truth Seeker Co.

Graham, L. (1975) <u>Deceptions and Myths of the Bible</u>. New York: Carol Publishing Group.

Graves, K. (1991) <u>The World's Sixteen Crucified Saviors</u>. New York: The Cleage Group.

Higgins, G. (1927) <u>Anacalypsis</u>. New Hyde Park, NY: University Books Inc.

Jackson, J.G. ((1972) <u>Man, God, and Civilization</u>. New York: University Books Inc.

Massey, G. (1992) <u>The Historical Jesus and the Mythical Christ.</u> Brooklyn, NY: A & B Books Publishing.

Shabazz, I.A. (1990) <u>Symbolism, Holidays, Myths, and Signs</u>. Jersey City: New Mind Productions.

Tardo, R.K. <u>The Shocking Truth About Christmas</u>. Arabi, Louisiana: Faithful World Publications.

CHRISTOPHER COLUMBUS

The original Haitians were called the Arawaks or Tainos. Christopher Columbus wrote in his log that the Arawaks were well built with good bodies and handsome features. He also reported that the Arawaks were remarkable for their hospitality and their belief in sharing. He said, "they offered to share with anyone and that when you ask for something they never say no." The Arawaks lived in village communes with a well-developed agriculture of corn, yams, and cassava. They had the ability to spin and weave, as well as being able to swim long distances. The Arawaks did not bear arms nor did they have prisons or prisoners. Columbus wrote that when the Santa Maria became shipwrecked, the Arawaks worked for hours to save the crew and cargo and that they were so honest that not one thing was missing. Arawak women were treated so well in early Haitian society that it startled the Spaniards. Columbus said that the Arawak men were of great intelligence because they could navigate all of their islands and give an amazingly precise account of everything.

The chief source, and on many matters the only source of information about what happened on the islands after Columbus arrived, was noted by a Catholic priest named Bartolome De Las Casas who lived during the time of Columbus. He transcribed Columbus' journal and wrote a multi-volume History of the Indies. Las Casas says that Columbus returned to America on his second voyage with seventeen ships and with more than 1200 heavily armed men with horses and attack dogs. Their aim was clearly to obtain as much gold and as many slaves as possible according to De Las Casas. Columbus went from island to island in the Caribbean, taking Arawaks as captives. He ordered everyone over the age of 14 to produce specific quantities of gold every three months, and if the Arawak could not produce this quota, Columbus then had his hands cut off; and left him to bleed to death.

CHRISTOPHER COLUMBUS.

If the Arawaks ever tried to escape, they were hunted down by the attack dogs and either hanged or burned alive. Within just two years, half of the three million Arawaks of Haiti died from murder, mutilation, or suicide. Bishop De Las Casas reported that the Spaniards became so lazy that they refused to walk any distance; and either rode the backs of the Arawaks or were carried on hammocks by Arawaks who ran them in relays. In other cases, the Spaniards had the Arawaks carry large leaves for their shade and had others to fan them with goose wings. Women were used as sex slaves and their children were murdered and then thrown into the sea. The Spaniards were so cruel, they thought nothing of cutting off slices of human flesh from the Arawaks just to test the sharpness of their blades. Bishop De Las Casas wrote, "My eyes have seen these acts so foreign to human nature that now I tremble as I write."

Christopher Columbus started the Trans-Atlantic slave trade by taking 500 of the healthiest men back to Spain to sell into slavery, and the proceeds from the sale helped to pay for his third voyage. The massive slave trade moving in the other direction, across the Atlantic from Africa to the Americas, was also begun in Haiti and was started by the son of Christopher Columbus in 1505 AD. On his third voyage to Haiti, Queen Isabelle's new Governor, Francisco De Bobadilla, had Christopher Columbus and his two brothers arrested and sent back to Spain in chains as prisoners for their crimes against the Arawaks.

Would Columbus Day still be celebrated if the real history of Christopher Columbus were told from the viewpoint of his victims?

REFERENCES AND ADDITIONAL READING

Blant, J.M. (1992) <u>1942: The Debate on Colonialism, Eurocenterism and History.</u> Trenton, NJ: African World Press Inc.

Bradley, M. (1992 <u>The Columbus Conspiracy.</u> Brooklyn, NY: A & B Books.

Carew, J. (1988) <u>Fulcrums of Change.</u> Trenton, NJ: African World Press.

Carew, J. (1994) <u>Rape of Paradise.</u> Brooklyn, NY: A & B Books.

Cohen, J.M. (ed.) (1969) <u>Christopher Columbus: The Four Voyages.</u> London: Penguin Books.

De Las Casas, B. (1971) <u>History of the Indies</u>. New York: Harper and Row.

Denevan, W. (ed.) (1976) <u>The Native Population of the Americas in 1492</u>. Madison: University of Wisconsin Press.

Konig, H. (1991) <u>Columbus: His Enterprise, Exploding the Myth</u>. New York: Monthly Review Press.

Mahtown, P. (1992) <u>Columbus: Sinking the Myth</u>. New York: World View Forum.

Nash, G. (1970) <u>Red, White, and Black: The People of Early America</u>. Englewood Cliffs: Prentice Hall.

Williams, E. ((1970) <u>From Columbus to Castro</u>. New York: Vintage Books.

Zinn, H. (1980) <u>A People's History of the United States</u>. New York: Harper Perennial.

BLACK INDIANS

Black Indian Chief

Black Indians, like other African Americans, have been treated by the writers of history as invisible. Two parallel institutions joined to create Black Indians: the seizure and mistreatment of Indians and their lands, and the enslavement of Africans. Today just about every African-American family tree has an Indian branch. Europeans forcefully entered the African blood stream, but Native Americans and Africans merged by choice, invitation and love. The two people discovered that they shared many vital views such as the importance of the family with children and the elderly being treasured. Africans and native Americans both cherished there own trustworthiness and saw promises and treaties as bonds never to be broken. Religion was a daily part of cultural life, not merely practiced on Sundays. Both Africans and Native Americans found they shared a belief in economic cooperation rather than competition and rivalry. Indians taught Africans techniques in fishing and hunting, and Africans taught Indians techniques in tropical agriculture and working in agricultural labor groups. Further, Africans had a virtual immunity to European diseases such as smallpox, which wiped out large communities of Native Americans.

The first recorded alliance in early America occurred on Christmas Day, 1522, when African and Indian slaves on a plantation owned by Christopher Columbus's son, rebelled and murdered their white masters. These Indian and African slaves escaped into the woods together and were never recaptured. Another successful alliance occurred around 1600, when runaway slaves and friendly Indians formed the Republic of Palmares in Northeastern Brazil, which successfully fought the Dutch and Portuguese for almost one hundred years. The Republic of Palmares grew to have one half-mile long streets that were six feet wide and lined with hundreds of homes, churches, and shops. Its well-kept lands produced cereals and crops irrigated by African style streams. The Republic was ruled by a king named "Ganga-Zumba," which combined the African word for great with the Indian word for ruler.

The history of the Saramaka people of Surinam in South America started around 1685, when African and Native American slaves escaped and together formed a maroon society, which fought with the Dutch for 80 years, until the Europeans abandoned their wars and sued for peace. Today the Saramakans total 20,000 people of mixed African-Indian ancestry.

By 1650, Mexico had a mixed African-Indian population of 100,000. Race mixing became so common in Mexico that the Spanish government passed laws prohibiting the two races from living together or marrying. In 1810, Vincente Guerrero of mixed African-Indian ancestry led the war for independence. In 1829, he became president of Mexico and immediately abolished slavery and the death sentence. He also began far reaching reforms including the construction of schools and libraries for the poor.

Escaped slaves became Spanish Florida's first settlers. They joined refugees from the Creek Nation and called themselves Seminoles, which means runaways.

There were three Seminole Wars.

Intermixing became so common that they were soon called Black Seminoles. Africans taught the Indians rice cultivation and how to survive in the tropical terrain of Florida. Eventually the Black Seminoles had well-built homes and raised fine crops of corn, sweet potatoes, and vegetables. They also owned large herds of live stock. The Black Seminoles struck frequently against slave plantations and runaway slaves swelled their ranks. The U.S. government launched three massive war campaigns against the Seminole nation over a period of 40 years. The second war alone cost the U.S. government over $40 million and 1,500 soldiers. The Seminoles eventually signed a peace treaty with President Polk, which was violated in 1849, when the U.S. Attorney General ruled that Black Seminoles were still slaves under U.S. law.

Black Indian societies were so common in every east coast state that by 1812, state legislatures began to remove the tax exemption status of Indian land by claiming that the tribes were no longer Indian. A Moravian missionary visited the Nanticoke nation on Maryland's eastern shore to compile a vocabulary of their language and found they were speaking pure African Mandingo.

After the Civil War, very few Blacks ever left their Indian nation because this was the only society that could guarantee that they would never be brutalized nor lynched. If Europeans had followed the wonderfully unique model of harmony, honesty, friendship, and loyalty exhibited by the African and Indian populations in North and South America, the "new world" could truly have been the land of the free, the home of the brave, and a place where "all men are created equal."

Chief Black Hair

REFERENCES AND ADDITIONAL READING

Albers, J. (1975) <u>Interaction of Color</u>. New Haven: Yale University Press.

Amos, A. & Senter, T. (eds.) (1996) <u>The Black Seminoles</u>. Gainesville: University Press of Florida.

Bailey, L. (1966) <u>Indian Slave Trade in the Southwest.</u> Los Angeles: Westernlore.

Bemrose, J . (1966) <u>Reminiscences of the Second Seminole War.</u> Gainesville: University Press of Florida.

Bowser, F. (1974) <u>The African Slave in Colonial Peru, 1524-1650.</u> Stanford: Stanford University Press.

Boxer, F. (1963) <u>Race Relations in the Portuguese Colonial Empire 1415-1825</u>. Oxford: Clarendon Press.

Cohen, D. & Greene, J. (eds.) <u>Neither Slave nor Free: The Freedman of African Descent in the Slave Societies of the New World.</u> Baltimore: Johns Hopkins.

Craven, W. (1971) <u>White, Red, and Black: The Seventeenth Century Virginian.</u> Charlottesville: University of Virginia Press.

Covington, J. (1982) <u>The Billy Bowlegs War: The Final Stand of the Seminoles against the Whites</u>. Cluluota, FL: Mickler House.

Forbes, J. (1993) <u>Africans and Native Americans</u>. Chicago: University of Illinois.

Forbes, J. (1964) <u>The Indian in America's Past.</u> Englewood Cliffs: Prentice Hall.

Katz, Loren (1986) <u>Black Indians</u>. New York: Macmillan Publishing Co.

Nash, G. (1970) <u>Red, White, and Black: The People of Early America.</u> Englewood Cliffs: Prentice Hall.

LORD DUNMORE'S ETHIOPIAN REGIMENT

Few textbooks acknowledge the tremendous contribution made by Black soldiers during the Revolutionary War. An even lesser known fact is that Black slaves also fought for the British in an attempt to win their freedom. Many slaves in fact were deceived by the British into thinking that American slavery would end if the British army defeated the American Continental Army. The British actually imprinted the inscription "Liberty to Slaves" across the chest of each Black volunteer soldier.

In November 1775, John Murray, the Earl of Dunmore and British Governor of Virginia, decided that the Revolutionary War would no longer continue as the "White man's war." Both the American and British senior strategists had banned the use of Black soldiers, but Lord Dunmore saw the British as hopelessly outnumbered and was unwilling to overlook any potential support. He also hoped a slave insurrection would deprive the American army of much needed labor for building fortifications and disrupt the American economy, since slave labor produced most of the cash crops. Lord Dunmore's proclamation declared "all indentured servants, Negroes, or others: FREE, that are able and willing to bear arms...to his Majesty's crown and dignity."

Dunmore's proclamation led Blacks to believe that the British were genuinely opposed to slavery. Since most American leaders such as George Washington and Thomas Jefferson were prominent slaveholders, many Blacks saw the British opportunity as their only chance for freedom and consequently joined the British in large numbers. J.A. Rogers states that "5,000 joined Dunmore at Norfolk; 25,000 fled from their masters in South Carolina and nearly seven-eights of the slaves in

Black Troops in Battle

Georgia." Nearly 2,000 slaves joined the British forces under General Cornwallis, including numerous slaves from George Washington's plantation. Thomas Jefferson declared that Virginia alone lost 30,000 and others estimate that as many as 100,000 slaves found their way to the British lines. One-half of Dunmore's troops that fought at Great Bridge on December 9, 1775 were runaway slaves.

Runaway slaves armed by the British are said to have terrorized the South. Many slaves overpowered their masters and handed their plantations over to the British. In the North, a strong garrison of Blacks known as the "Negro Fort", defeated their former masters in a battle in the Bronx, New York City. Other Blacks joined the British Navy as seamen and pilots and successfully stole American ships and attacked numerous coastal towns. During the sieges of Charleston and

Savannah, thousands of Black laborers built fortifications, while others in Virginia constructed two dams. Blacks also served as guides, spies, and intelligence agents for the invading British armies. Ex-slave Thomas Johnson claimed to have conducted the detachment which surprised Colonial Washington at Monks Corner. The British even created a Black cavalry troop in 1782. British General William Phillips commented: "These Negroes have undoubtedly been of the greatest use."

George Washington told Congress that "Dunmore's appeal made him the most formidable enemy America has; and his strength will increase like a snowball by rolling and faster if some expedient cannot be hit upon to convince the slaves and servants of the impotency of his designs." American slaveholders were still unwilling to arm their slaves until all other countermeasures were tried. Highway and river patrols were instituted to capture runaway slaves. Vigorous anti-British propaganda was circulated and Southern slaves were frequently hidden in mines to avoid British capture. Several Southern states even approved the death penalty for recaptured slaves, but nothing could stop the Black contributions to the British war effort. General Washington wrote Colonel Henry Lee on December 20, 1775: "We must use the Negroes or run the risk of losing the war...success will depend on which side can arm the Negroes faster."

The Continental army finally agreed to accept African American volunteers (both slave and free) when the desertion rate of White soldiers began to reach enormous proportions. Washington complained: "The lack of patriotism is infinitely more to be dreaded than the whole of Great Britain assisted by Negro allies." Once freedom was promised, African Americans showed the real "Spirit of '76" and joined the Continental army in such massive numbers that General Schuyler wrote: "Is it consistent with the sons of freedom to trust their all to be defended by slaves?" On October 23, 1777, a British officer named Schlozer wrote: "The Negro can take the field instead of his master and therefore no regiment is to be seen in which there are not Negroes in abundance and among them are able-bodied, strong, and brave fellows." Sir Henry Clinton wrote Lord Germaine, British Minister of State: "It is safe to say that but for the aid of the Negro, independence would not have been won."

The American victory required the evacuation of all persons who had been loyal to the British. About 27,000 White Loyalists were relocated to Nova Scotia, Canada, but the majority of the Black Loyalists were betrayed by the British government, which sold almost all of the former slaves back into slavery. Only the original 3,500 Black soldiers who became "Lord Dunmore's Ethiopian Regiment" were relocated to Nova Scotia. Although they were promised land and provisions, most Blacks received neither and became beggars or cheap laborers for White Loyalists who were given farms as large as 200 acres by the government with free provisions for three years. When a London based abolition group headed by John Clarkson offered the Black Loyalists a new home in Africa, over 1,200 sailed in 15 crowded ships for Sierra Leone on January 15, 1792, where they founded the capital city of Freetown. The Nova Scotians eventually embraced and intermarried with the African community and provided the core of what became the national culture, language, and early leadership of Sierra Leone. However, more than two centuries later, their descendants still identify themselves as Nova Scotians and the direct descendants of "Lord Dunmore's Ethiopian Regiment".

REFERENCES AND ADDITIONAL READING

Aptheker, H. (1940) <u>The Negro in the American Revolution</u>. New York.

Armstrong, M. (1948) <u>The Great Awakening in Nova Scotia, 1766-1809.</u> Hartford.

Banton, M. (1957) <u>West African City: A Study of Tribal Life in Freetown</u>. London.

Beck, M. (1957) <u>The Government of Nova Scotia.</u> Toronto.

Bennett, L. (1988) <u>Before the Mayflower</u>. New York.

Butt-Thompson, F. (1926) <u>Sierra Leone in History and Tradition</u>. London.

Clairmont, D. (1970) <u>Nova Scotian Blacks: An Historical and Structural Overview</u>. Halifax.

Clendenen, C. & Duigan, P. (1964) <u>Americans in Black Africa up to 1865</u>. Stanford.

Crooks, J. (1903) <u>A History of the Colony of Sierra Leone, West Africa.</u> Dublin.

Davis, D. (1966) <u>The Problem of Slavery in Western Culture.</u> New York.

Elkins, S. (1959) <u>Slavery: A Problem in American Institutional and Intellectual Life.</u> New York.

Franklin, J. (1969) <u>From Slavery to Freedom.</u> New York.

Rogers, J. (1989) <u>Africa's Gift to America.</u> St. Petersburg, FL.

Walker, J. (1992) <u>The Black Loyalists</u>. Toronto.

CHRISTOPHER COLUMBUS VS BELGIUM KING LEOPOLD II

In trying to determine the worse human rights violator over the past 500 years, two candidates far and away exceed all others. Adolph Hitler was not even close because he is only credited with killing six million people and his reign of terror only lasted about six years. Over a period of 25 years, Belgium King Leopold II was able to reduce the population of the Congo from 20 million to 10 million. 25 years after Christopher Columbus entered Haiti, the Arawak population was reduced to zero, that is, total annihilation or genocide.

In describing the exploits of Columbus, Dominican priest Bartolome de Las Casas wrote: "My eyes have seen these acts so foreign to human nature that I tremble as I write." Famous American author Joseph Conrad called Leopold's Congo: "The vilest scramble for loot that ever disfigured the history of human conscience." Despite a death toll of holocaust dimensions, these men are not even mentioned in the standard litany of human horrors. Our children are given history books that describe Columbus as a heroic adventurer and an outstanding seaman. This heroic image is further perpetuated by Columbus Day celebrations and the fact that streets, schools, cities, and even countries have been named after him. King Leopold II enjoys an equally positive reputation. Belgium history describes him as a "philanthropic monarch who was much admired throughout Europe." He is praised for investing a large portion of his personal fortune in pubic works projects to benefit both Europe and Africa. The current image of these two men could not be further from the truth! Both left behind a heritage of racism, greed, hunger, exploitation, and genocide. Leopold matched Columbus so closely in atrocities that one has to wonder whether they represent the same man reincarnated.

Both Columbus and Leopold were great salesmen and great liars. To help finance his second voyage, Columbus told the Spanish Monarch that "there are many wide rivers of which the majority contain gold...there are many spices, and great mines of gold and other metals." Columbus was so convincing that Queen Isabella provided him with 17 ships and 1,200 men for his second voyage, and promised him 10% of all the gold and precious metals he brought back. Leopold's opportunity for salesmanship and lying came at the Berlin Conference (November 1884 - February 1885) where European countries met to decide how they would divide up Africa. Leopold begged for the Congo Basin and guaranteed the well being of the Congo's native population. Leopold told the American delegation that "Belgium deserves the opportunity to prove to the world that it also was an imperial people, capable of dominating and enlightening others." Since Leopold knew that the Belgium parliament and Belgium people had no interest in Africa, he essentially was arguing for a land mass 80 times the size of Belgium, which he would own personally.

Columbus and Leopold saw the profits from their new lands as virtually limitless if enough free labor were available. Both men immediately proceeded to institute slavery among the native population and set quotas for individual production. The favorite method of punishment by Columbus and Leopold for not meeting quotas was to cut off the hands.

Columbus ordered all persons 14 years and older to collect a certain quantity of gold every three months. When they brought it, they were given copper tokens to hang around their necks. Arawaks found without copper tokens to hang around their necks had their hands cut off and bled to death. Leopold chose to set quotas for ivory and rubber for each village. When a village fell short of its quota, his soldiers brutally raided the village and cut off the victims' right hands. Sean Kelly wrote: "Hands became a sort of currency in that soldiers were paid their bonuses on the basis of how many right hands they collected."

Belgium King Leopold II

Columbus and Leopold were exceptionally cruel to women and children. Both men allowed their soldiers to kidnap women as sex slaves, and they also held women and children as hostages to insure that the native men would not run away. Female hostages were usually poorly fed and large numbers died of starvation. Newborns also had a very high mortality rate because the mothers were too famished to provide nursing milk.

The Arawaks and Africans both fought back but were no match for the armor and swords of Columbus nor the guns and artillery of Leopold's soldiers. Rebelling natives were treated exceedingly cruel by both oppressors. Although both men used hanging, Columbus preferred burning victims alive if possible or feeding them to the attack dogs. Leopold's soldiers enjoyed summary executions

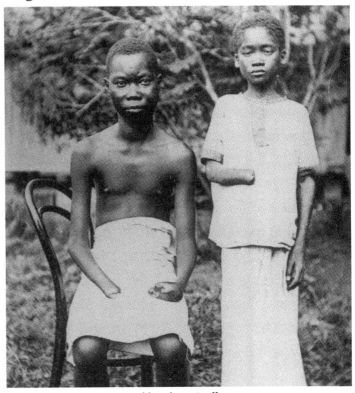
Hands cut off

followed by chopping off the victims' heads and placing the heads on poles around their gardens. Guillaume Van Kerckhoven, a Leopold officer, cheerfully bragged to a missionary that he paid his Black soldiers five brass rods per human head they brought him during the course of any military operation he conducted. He said it was to stimulate their prowess in the face of the enemy.

A single man in both cases dedicated his life to exposing the atrocities of Columbus and Leopold to the world. Bartolome de Las Casas, a Dominican priest, was initially a friend of Columbus and helped transcribe his journals. However, he soon became a vehement critic of Spanish cruelty and published a two-volume book detailing Spanish torture. He estimates that three million Arawaks died between 1495 and 1508. Edmund Dene Morel, a trusted employee of the Liverpool shipping line, dedicated his life to exposing the atrocities of King Leopold. He single-handedly put this subject on the world's front pages for more than a decade, which resulted in worldwide protest rallies. Morel mobilized everyone from Booker T. Washington to the Archbishop of Canterbury to join his cause. He even went to the White House insisting to President Theodore Roosevelt that the United States had a special responsibility to do something about the Congo, since the U.S. helped Leopold at the Berlin Conference. Morel's unrelenting efforts resulted in Western powers forcing King Leopold to sell the Congo to Belgium in 1908.

Despite responsibility for death tolls of holocaust dimensions, neither Christopher Columbus nor King Leopold II was convicted or imprisoned for any crimes. Both men lived a full life and died exceptionally rich. Columbus spent his last years living in a mansion in Valladolid with an annual income of $60,000 from his Hispaniola sugar plantations (a fortune in the 1500s). Leopold died in 1909 with a personal fortune (produced by the Congo's ivory and rubber) of well over a billion dollars in today's currency.

Willie "C" Jackson
1531 W. 64th Street
Los Angeles CA. 90047

In order to prevent the human atrocities of Columbus and Leopold from ever reoccurring, it might be prudent to adopt the current philosophy regarding Adolph Hitler; that is, constant reminders of the holocausts in newspapers, magazines, books, radio, television, and even holocaust museums followed by the statement: "Never Again".

Millions of children saw their parents murdered by King Leopold's soldiers.

REFERENCES AND ADDITIONAL READING

Anstey, R. (1966) <u>King Leopold's Legacy: The Congo Under Belgian Rule 1908-1960.</u> London: Oxford University Press.

Bauer, L. (1935) <u>Leopold the Unloved: King of the Belgians and of Wealth</u>. Boston: Little, Brown, and Co.

Blant, J.M. (1992) <u>1942: The Debate on Colonialism, Eurocenterism and History.</u> Trenton, NJ: African World Press Inc.

Bradley, M. (1992 <u>The Columbus Conspiracy.</u> Brooklyn, NY: A & B Books.

Carew, J. (1994) <u>Rape of Paradise</u>. Brooklyn, NY: A & B Books.

Cohen, J.M. (ed.) (1969) <u>Christopher Columbus: The Four Voyages.</u> London: Penguin Books.

De Las Casas, B. (1971) <u>History of the Indies</u>. New York: Harper and Row.

Emerson, B. (1979) <u>Leopold II of the Belgiums: King of Colonialism</u>. London: Weidenfield and Nicolson.

Fetter, B. (1983) <u>Colonial Rule and Regional Imbalance in Central Africa.</u> Boulder, CO: Westview Press.

Gann, L. & Duignan, P. (1979) <u>The Rulers of Belgium Africa 1884-1914.</u> Princeton: Princeton University Press.

Hochschild, A. (1998) <u>King Leopold's Ghost</u>. New York: Houghton Mifflin Co.

BLACKS AND THE REVOLUTIONARY WAR

African American participation was enormous during the events leading to American Independence, but these contributions are seldom mentioned in contemporary history books. For example, Crispus Attucks, a Black man and probably an escaped slave, was the first person killed in Boston when tensions between British soldiers and an angry crowd resulted in the death of five people. March 5, 1770, was initially called the day of the Boston Massacre but the name was soon changed to Crispus Attucks Day. Crispus Attucks Day remained the chief American anniversary until independence was won and it was replaced by July 4. John Adams, our second president, called March 5, 1770, the most important event in American history. On October 13, 1888, a monument was erected on Boston Common called the Crispus Attucks Memorial.

Death of Crispus Attucks

Cripus Attucks Monument in Boston

British resentment increased dramatically after the Boston Massacre until things finally exploded on April 19, 1775, into the Revolutionary War. At least a dozen Black militiamen were among those firing the "shots heard round the world" at Lexington on April 19. One of the first Americans to fall was a Black minuteman named Prince Estabrook. The second major clash was fought at Bunker Hill on June 17, where two African Americans again became great heroes. Peter Salem became famous after he shot and killed Major Pitcairn, the British commander. Salem Poor so distinguished himself in this same battle that 13 officers including his commander, Colonel Brewer, recommended him for official recognition to the General Court of Massachusetts.

The Battle of Bunker Hill where Peter Salem, pictured at the far right, killed Major Pitcairn the British commander.

However, less than 6 months after Lexington and the Battle of Bunker Hill, a pattern of exclusion of Blacks from the new nation's military units had begun to develop. Southern slave owners protested vehemently against the use of Black people in the Revolutionary War including George Washington who himself was a slave owner. Finally, on October 8, 1775, Continental Army headquarters bowed to Southern pressure and issued a decree excluding all African Americans from service in Continental units.

As the war dragged on and the number of White deserters became enormous, Washington complained that "the lack of patriotism is infinitely more to be dreaded than the whole British army." Washington changed his mind drastically after his defeat by the British at New York, when he was greatly outnumbered. He then partitioned the new government to welcome all able-bodied men into the Continental Army whether Black or White, slave or free. Accordingly, on March 14, 1779, Alexander recommended that South Carolina and Georgia " take measures for raising 3,000 able-bodied Negroes who would receive no pay but would be emancipated at the end of the war." White slave masters of the North and South who didn't want to risk their lives, or their sons' lives were allowed to send slaves to take their place. There were soon so many Black soldiers that General Schuyler wrote "is it consistent with the sons of freedom to trust their ALL to be defended by slaves?" Nineteenth century American historian, Ben J. Lossing, wrote that "as the war went on, and the ranks of the army grew thinner, an increasing number of Negroes took the place of the Whites, until it began to appear that Ethiopia as well as America was in arms." Baron Von Clausen stated that of the 20,000 men he saw with Washington in January, 1781, "5000 were Negroes."

It is indisputable that African Americans provided the balance of power that brought America independence. They distinguished themselves in every possible manner from combat soldier to support personnel who built virtually every fortification and new building from Vermont to South Carolina.   Sir Henry

Clinton wrote Lord Germaine, British Minister of State, "it is safe to say that but for the aid of the Negro, independence would not have been won." All Black regiments as well as soldiers who distinguished themselves were mentioned by the hundreds. Rhode Island, with a small population and two thirds of its territory occupied by the British, became the first colony to authorize the enlistment of all slave regiments. At the battle of Rhode Island, August 27, 1778, a regiment of 226 slaves repelled a force of 6,000 British who charged them three times in an attempt to dislodge them from a strategic valley. Dr. Harris wrote "they preserved our army from capture and helped gain our liberty." General Lafayette called this "the best action of the whole war."

A company of Blacks from Boston called the "Bucks of America" rendered such valuable service that John Hancock gave them a special flag and honored them with a special affair at Boston. George Bancroft wrote of the Battle of Monmouth in New Jersey in 1778, "may history record that more than 700 Black men offered their lives for their country and fought side by side with Whites." Commander Nathaniel Shaler thought so highly of the Black soldiers who fought under him that he sent a letter to Governor Thompkins stating that "they ought to be registered in the book of fame and remembered as long as bravery is considered a virtue."

In general, the contributions of Black Americans who had fought to bring freedom to America were not forgotten. Virtually all of the slaves who fought in the war received their freedom after the war. In fact, the institution of slavery did not even last throughout the war in most northern states. In 1777, Vermont became the first state to abolish slavery. Pennsylvania followed in 1780, and Massachusetts in 1783. Rhode Island freed its slaves in 1784. Even Virginia passed a law freeing all slaves who participated in the war. Unfortunately, the contributions of African Americans were soon forgotten in the South, where the vast majority of them lived, and the institution of slavery soon returned to business as usual.

REFERENCES AND ADDITIONAL READING

Aptheker, H. (1974) <u>A Documentary History of the Negro People in the United States.</u>
Secaucus, NJ: Citadel Press.

Bailyn, B. & Garrett, N (eds.) (1965) <u>Pamphlets of the American Revolution</u>. Cambridge:
Harvard University Press.

Becker, C. (1958) <u>The Declaration of Independence: A Study in the History of Political</u>
<u>Ideas</u>. New York: Random House.

Degler, C. (1970) <u>Out of Our Past</u>. New York: Harper and Row.

Hill, C. (1964) <u>Puritanism and Revolution</u>. New York: Schocken.

Kurtz, S. & Hutson, J. (eds.) <u>Essays on the American Revolution</u>. Chapel Hill: University of
North Carolina.

Lynd, S. (1967) <u>Class Conflict, Slavery, and the Constitution</u>. Indianapolis: Bobbs-Merrill.

Maier, P. (1972) <u>From Resistance to Revolution: Colonial Radicals and the Development of</u>
<u>American Opposition to Britain, 1765-1776</u>. New York: Knopf.

Shy, J. (1976) <u>A People Numerous and Armed: Reflections on the Military Struggle for</u>
<u>American Independence.</u> New York: Oxford University Press.

Smith, P. (1976) <u>A New Age Now Begins: A People's History of the American Revolution.</u>
New York: McGraw-Hill.

Young, A. (ed.) (1976) <u>The American Revolution: Explorations in the History of American</u>
<u>Radicalism</u>. DeKalb, Illinois: Northern Illinois University Press.

Zinn, H. (1980) <u>A People's History of the United States</u>. New York: Harper Perennial.

AFRICAN WARRIOR:
QUEEN NZINGA

Queen Nzinga

Nzinga (1582-1663) became queen of what is now called Angola in 1623, and dedicated her entire life to fighting the Portuguese to prevent the enslavement of her people. She proved to be a cunning rival to the Portuguese and became famous for her intelligence, bravery, and brilliant military strategies, which were imitated for centuries during struggles for independence throughout Africa.

In the 16th century, the Portuguese stake in the slave trade was threatened by England, France, and the Dutch. This caused the Portuguese to transfer their slave-trading activities southward to the Congo and to Southwest Africa. Their most stubborn opposition, as they entered the final phase of the conquest of Angola, came from a queen who became a legendary head of state and military leader with few peers in world history.

Jesuit Priests performed mass baptisms on slave ship decks

Nzinga was one of five children born to her powerful father, King (or ngola) Kiluanji of Ndongo -which the Portuguese called Angola after the word for king: ngola. The Mbundu tribe of King Kiluanji initially welcomed the Portuguese as trading partners. In fact, King Kiluanji became wealthy and powerful enough through Portuguese trading that he conquered all the surrounding territories.

Subsequently, disputes over these new territories created the rift that eventually ended the Portuguese alliance. King Kiluanji was such a great fighter that he was able to repel the early Portuguese invasions of the border territories. When Kiluanji died, his eldest son Mbandi declared himself king. Mbandi, however, greatly feared the Portuguese guns and canons and when they advanced, he fled to an island on the Cuanza River and asked his sister Nzinga to negotiate a peace treaty with the Portuguese governor. The arrogant Portuguese had been appointing governors over Angola for over forty years without having control.

Nzinga's 1622 negotiating conference with the new governor, Joao Correa DeSouza, has become a legend in the history of Africa's confrontation with Europe. Despite the fact that her brother had surrendered everything to the Portuguese, Nzinga arrived as a royal negotiator rather than a humble conquered messenger. When the governor only provided one chair for himself, she summoned one of her women, who provided a royal carpet and then fell to her hands and knees to become a human seat. When Governor DeSouza entered, he found himself already out maneuvered. When the governor asked for the release of all Portuguese war prisoners, Nzinga smilingly agreed, provided all her Mbundu people, who had been carried off to Brazil and elsewhere, were brought back in exchange. This condition was eventually reduced to returning Portuguese prisoners in exchange for allowing her brother, King Mbandi, to remain ruler of an independent Ndongo kingdom and withdrawing the Portuguese army. Nzinga made it clear she would only negotiate a treaty on equal terms.

Probably as part of a private agreement intended to reinforce the treaty, Nzinga stayed in town and became baptized as "Anna" in the Christian faith. Such a move was more political than religious because Nzinga knew that even her father had opposed the mass conversion to Christianity of the Mbundu. She knew that the Jesuit priests ran the slave trade for the Portuguese. They sprinkled "Holy Water" while officiating at daily mass baptisms on the docks, where lines of captives shuffled into slave ships with such names as "Jesus" and "John the Baptist". Nzinga also knew that her status as a "Christian" ally of Portugal would entitle her people to favored status. She was even politically astute enough to allow herself the full Christian name of Dona Anna DeSouza in order to strengthen her links with the governor.

Shortly after negotiating with Nzinga, Governor DeSouza was replaced by a new governor after quarreling with the Jesuit priests. The new governor promptly broke all the treaty agreements. Nzinga demanded that her brother, King Mbandi, declare war on the Portuguese. Unfortunately, cowardly King Mbandi had no such intentions and went to the Portuguese asking for protection against Nzinga and to re-enforce his authority over his own people. Nzinga, now determined to do away with this treacherous weakling, had him killed and then promptly declared war on the Portuguese herself. She initially trained an all female army which repeatedly defeated the Portuguese using guerrilla style tactics. She then recruited neighboring tribes and also allied with the Dutch. The Dutch military attache who accompanied her reported that the people loved Nzinga so much that everyone fell to their knees and kissed the ground as she approached. He believed that all were willing to die under her leadership. The Portuguese retreated to their strongholds and forts on the coast giving the Dutch threat as an excuse and not the threat of being annihilated by the queen's forces. Nzinga's main goal was always to end the enslavement of her people. She even sent word throughout Africa in 1624, that any slave who could make it to her territory was henceforth and forever free. This act alone should make Nzinga one of the greatest women in history because there was no other place on the continent of Africa that offered such freedom.

The Portuguese responded to this threat by calling in a massive force of men and artillery from their colony of Brazil. Nzinga's guerrilla warfare tactics for resisting the well armed Portuguese soldiers have been much admired and even imitated successfully in this century. Since the Portuguese used large numbers of Black

Nzinga's goal was to end African enslavement

soldiers, she became the first Black leader and most successful, to carefully organize efforts to undermine and destroy the effective employment of Black soldiers by Whites. She instructed her soldiers to infiltrate the Portuguese by allowing themselves to become recruited by Portuguese agents. Once members of the Portuguese military, her soldiers would encourage rebellion and desertion by the Black troops which frequently resulted in whole companies of Portuguese soldiers joining Nzinga along with much needed guns and ammunition. This quiet and effective work of Nzinga's agents among the Black troops of Portugal is one of the most glorious, yet unsung, pages of African history. The Portuguese generals frequently complained that they never knew which Black soldier was friend or foe.

When the massive Portuguese manpower and firepower began to gain the upper hand, she sent word throughout Angola that she had died in order to stop the Portuguese offensive. While pretending to have died in Angola, Nzinga moved east to the neighboring country of Matamba where she defeated the ruling queen and created a new land for herself, her people, and all escaped slaves. She consolidated her power in Matamba and then began sending out war parties from Matamba to attack any settlement or tribe that had aided the Portuguese. In 1629, the Portuguese stood shocked when Queen Nzinga "burst upon them from the grave" recapturing large segments of her own country. She was now queen of both Matamba and Ndongo and redoubled her efforts against slavery by dealing ruthlessly with any Black chief found participating in the slave trade.

Nzinga never stopped resisting the powerful Portuguese even as she approached her 80th birthday. She was called the "Black Terror" by the Portuguese and was clearly the greatest adversary and military strategist that ever confronted the armed forces of Portugal. Her tactics kept the Portuguese commanders in confusion and dismay and her constant aim was never less than the total destruction of the slave trade. The long guerrilla campaign that led to Angola's independence 300 years later was continuously inspired by the queen who never surrendered.

REFERENCES AND ADDITIONAL READING

Hyman, M. (1994) <u>Blacks Before America.</u> Trenton, NJ: Africa World Press.

Jackson, J. (1970) <u>Introduction to African Civilization</u>. New York: Carol Publishing Group.

Robinson, C. & Battle, R. (1987) <u>The Journey of the Songhai People.</u> Philadelphia: Farmer Press.

Rogers, J. (1972) <u>World's Great Men of Color.</u> New York: Macmillan Publishing Co.

Sweetman, D. (1971) <u>Queen Nzinga.</u> London: Longman.

Sweetman, D. (1984) <u>Women Leaders in African History.</u> Portsmouth, New Hampshire: Heinemann Educational Books.

Van Sertima, I. (1988) <u>Black Women in Antiquity</u>. New Brunswick, NJ: Transaction Publishers.

Williams, C. (1987) <u>The Destruction of Black Civilization</u>. Chicago: Third World Press.

Woodson, C. (1969) <u>African Heroes and Heroines</u>. Washington, DC: The Associated Publishers Inc.

SLAVE CHILDREN OF THOMAS JEFFERSON

In the 1860 census in the South, there were 500,000 mulatto or mixed race slaves and 350,000 slave owners. Thus, every slave owner had on average produced more than one slave child. The slave children of former President Thomas Jefferson, and their direct descendants, are among the most carefully studied families in the history of America because of their outstanding achievements up to, and including, Chairman of the Board of Du Pont Chemical Corporation.

Thomas Jefferson is considered the greatest and most brilliant statesman this country has ever produced. Moreover, among the founding fathers, he was the one who was the most vocal opponent of slavery and did the most to contribute to its abolition. He wrote the Declaration of Independence with a clause opposing slavery, which was taken out at the insistence of the other signers. He wrote the Northwest Ordinance in 1783, and included a clause that prohibited slavery in the new areas of Ohio, Indiana, and Illinois. Jefferson negotiated the Louisiana Purchase from France in 1803, and included a provision, which prohibited the introduction of slavery into these new areas. While president, Thomas Jefferson pushed through Congress a bill in 1808, which prohibited the importation of slaves, and authorized the U.S. Navy to seize and confiscate ships containing slaves on the high seas. Thomas Jefferson was married to Martha Wayles, the daughter of John Wayles, for 10 years before she died in 1776. Upon the death of Martha Wayles and her father, Jefferson inherited 11,000 acres of land and 135 slaves. Sally Hemmings was one of the slaves inherited. She was also a daughter of John Wayles and an African slave, and thus his wife's half sister. Jefferson fell in love with this mulatto slave after she accompanied his daughter to France, where he was U.S. Ambassador in 1787. Their first son "Tom" was born in 1789. Sally Hemmings produced Beverly Hemmings in 1798, while Thomas Jefferson was Vice President, and three other children while Jefferson was President, including Harriet in 1801, Madison in 1805, and Eston in 1808.

Thomas Jefferson

Beverly and Harriet Hemmings were allowed to run away in 1822. Harriet married a White person, and never acknowledged her parents. Beverly ended up in England, where he also passed for White. His great-grandson, Edward Graham Jefferson, migrated back to the U.S. and became a naturalized American citizen. He subsequently became CEO of Du Pont Chemical Corporation, retiring in 1986 and was a member of the Board at AT&T Corporation, Chemical Bank, and Seagram Corporation.

Sally Hemmings' first son, Tom, eventually married Jemima, the slave daughter of a master named Drury Woodson, and changed his name to Tom Woodson. He became the distributor of an abolitionist newspaper and a leader in the Black community. Federal Judge Timothy Lewis in 1991, became the first prominent person to admit publicly that he was a descendant of Sally Hemmings and son, Tom Woodson. This was only after his Senate confirmation hearings. Most descendants were ashamed of their slave ancestry.

Monticello

Frederick Madison Roberts, the grandson of Madison Hemmings, became the first Black man ever elected to the State Assembly of California. He also became a close friend of Earl Warren and helped found UCLA, that is, the University of California at Los Angeles. Sally Hemmings' last-born son, Eston, had a son named John Wayles Jefferson who founded the Continental Cotton Company, which was very successful.

Thomas Jefferson was the most vocal opponent against slavery and spent his entire life working for the abolition of slavery. He strongly believed that "all men are created equal" and that they could achieve equally if only given the opportunity. Jefferson would be proud to know that his slave children confirmed his theory about racial equality by their outstanding achievements.

REFERENCES AND ADDITIONAL READING

Adler, D. (1987) <u>Thomas Jefferson: Father of our Democracy</u>. New York: Holiday House.

Bakhufu, A. (1993) <u>The Six Black Presidents</u>. Washington, D.C.: PIK2 Publications.

Bear, J. & Betts, E. (1987) <u>Thomas Jefferson's Farm Book.</u> University Press of Virginia.

Bennett, L. (1988) <u>Before the Mayflower.</u> New York: Penguin Books.

Brodie , F. (1974) <u>Thomas Jefferson, An Intimate History</u>. New York: W.W. Norton & Co.

Erikson, E. (1974) <u>Dimensions of a New Identity: Jefferson Lectures</u>. New York: W.W. Norton & Co.

Jefferson, I. (1951) <u>Memoirs of a Monticello Slave</u>. University of Virginia.

Kane, J. (1981) <u>Facts About the Presidents: From George Washington to Ronald Reagan</u>. New York: The H.W. Wilson Co.

Malone, D. (1981) <u>Jefferson and His Times: The Sage of Monticello</u>. Boston: Little, Brown, & Co.

Mapp, A. (1987) <u>Thomas Jefferson: A Strange Case of Mistaken Identity</u>. New York: Madison Books.

Reuter, E. (1969) <u>The Mulatto in the United States</u>. Haskell House.

Sloan, S. (1992) <u>The Slave Children of Thomas Jefferson</u>. Berkeley: The Orsden Press.

Sullivan, M. (1991) <u>Presidential Passions: The Love Affairs of America's Presidents-From Washington and Jefferson to Kennedy and Johnson.</u> New York: Shapolsky Publishers Inc.

Tinsell, C. (1964) <u>The Secret Loves of the Founding Fathers.</u> New York: Devin-Adair Co.

PAUL CUFFE: AMERICA'S RICHEST AFRICAN AMERICAN

Paul Cuffe (1759-1817) was the richest African American in the United States during the early 1800s, but never stopped championing the cause of better conditions for his people. At the age of 19, he sued the Massachusetts courts for the right to vote stating that taxation without representation should be illegal. He built on his own farm, New Bedford's only school for the children of "free Negroes" and personally sponsored their teachers. He authored the first document of its kind addressed to the New Jersey Legislature asking that body "to petition the Congress of the United States that every slave be freed and that every Colored man that so desired be allowed to leave America." By 1811, Paul Cuffe finally concluded that if the richest Black person in America was considered a second class citizen, then emigration back to Africa was the only answer for Black social, economic, and political self-determination. On December 12, 1815, Cuffe personally sponsored and transported nine families (38 people) back to Africa in what he hoped would be the first of many such voyages.

Paul Cuffe was one of ten children born to a slave father, Saiz Kufu (later, Cuffe) and an Indian mother. The father was freed by his Quaker master in 1745, and earned enough money working for ship owners to buy a 116-acre farm in Dartmouth, Massachusetts. in 1766. Paul left the farming to his siblings and chose a maritime life and by age 14 was working full time on whaling ships. By age 18, he had become so thoroughly self-taught in mathematics, navigation, and other seafaring skills that he decided to build his own boat for self-employment. During the Revolutionary War, he made enough money smuggling goods past British blockade patrol ships that he was able to purchase a shipyard and construct three small whaling boats between 1787 and 1795. During one season alone,

In 1811 Paul Cuffe and his Black crew sailed to Sierra Leone to investigate the possibility of repatriating African Americans to that African country. This engraved silhouette, dated 1812, commemorated that voyage.

Cuffe and his crew captured six whales and Cuffe proved his courage and commitment by asking his crew to lower him to the side of the boat where he personally harpooned two whales.

Paul Cuffe's early activity was fraught with danger as he purchased and delivered freight along the Atlantic seaboard. Pirates were a constant threat and on more than one occasion his ship was captured and all of his merchandise stolen, but he never stopped pursuing his dream. The Fugitive Slave Act was also a constant threat, especially since Cuffe exclusively staffed his businesses and ships with Blacks to demonstrate their equality and to reinforce their self-confidence and sense of racial pride. The Fugitive Slave Act legalized the seizure of any Black person suspected of escape from slavery by any White person. Since African Americans could not testify in court, "the Black accused would have to find, and persuade a White person to appear at his trial and convince the authorities that the accused was free" or risk being resold into slavery. Moreover, Paul Cuffe was once arrested for several days and his boat seized during a delivery to Vienna, Maryland by Federal Collector of Customs, James Frazier. In 1796, Maryland had passed a law "requiring any 'suspicious' free Black to six months of servitude." Since a vessel owned and operated by Blacks was unprecedented, it was certainly "suspicious". Whites were also concerned about what this demonstration of Black achievement might have on otherwise obedient slaves. However, Cuffe had "impeccable mercantile credentials, proof of registry at Bedford, Massachusetts, and receipts from such reliable merchant houses as William Rotch and Sons."

As the Cuffe commercial enterprises continued to prosper, he expanded by purchasing a 200-acre farm, a gristmill, and by building ships large enough to enable him to purchase and deliver freight internationally. In 1800, Cuffe built the 162-ton "Hero" which sailed around Africa's Cape of Good Hope eight times while delivering merchandise from Portuguese East Africa to Europe. Paul Cuffe's largest ship was the 268-ton "Alpha," which Cuffe and nine Black crew members sailed from Savannah, Georgia to Gothenburg, Sweden with a large cargo in 1806.

Despite the fact that Paul Cuffe was the richest Black man and largest Black employer in America, he was convinced that no amount of wealth would make a Black man socially acceptable in America and that Blacks would always be "resident aliens". He felt the only answer was to develop a strong Black African nation. Cuffe declared: "Blacks would be better off in Africa, where we could rise to be a people." When William Rotch told him of a British program to repatriate unwanted Blacks living in London to Sierra Leone, he immediately sailed to England for more information. Cuffe hoped that a strong Black nation could trade with Great Britain and the United States and that educated "free Negroes" from America could provide the much-needed technology. American technology was needed because a British law (1731) forbad any White person from teaching any Black person a trade, thus reducing London's "Black Poor" to unemployable beggars whom the government wanted sent to Africa.

While traveling to England and Sierra Leone, Paul Cuffe used an introductory letter from President Thomas Jefferson to help him gather data on manufacturing, operating costs, threatening colonial practices, and available trade opportunities. Cuffe found the residents of Sierra Leone very receptive to his prescription for reviving Black industry. They also hoped that a strong economic and social return of Africa to its past glory would help dissuade the slave trade. A large percentage of the population of Freetown were former American slaves who had fought with the British during the Revolutionary War and then were evacuated to Nova Scotia, Canada with the White British Loyalists. Both severe racism and severe climate encouraged the Black Nova Scotians to leave en-mass for Sierra Leone in November 1792. Paul Cuffe hired Aaron Richards, a Black settler in Freetown, as the captain's apprentice "to prepare the road to progress," and before leaving, Cuffe founded the "Friendly Society for the Emigration of Free Negroes from America." After his return to America, "Cuffe began a speaking tour to introduce free Blacks to the notion of nation building in Africa."

The War of 1812 interrupted Cuffe's trade and emigration plans until 1815, at which time he paid $4,000 from personal funds to transport 38 African Americans to Sierra Leone, where he then successfully secured homesteads for all of his Black American brethren, at his own expense. Failing health prevented any future trips and Cuffe died on September 9, 1817. Paul Cuffe's legacy is not as a wealthy Black man but as a wealthy Black man who fought for the betterment of his people and was always willing to back his convictions with self-sacrifice, discipline, determination, and financial resources.

REFERENCES AND ADDITIONAL READING

Adams, R. (1969) <u>Great Negroes: Past and Present.</u> Chicago: Afro-Am Publishing Co. Inc.

Al-Mansour, K. (1993) <u>Betrayal by Any Other Name</u>. San Francisco: The First African Arabian Press.

Appiah, K. & Gates, H. (eds.) (1999) <u>Africana.</u> New York: Basis Civitas Books.

Aptheker, H. (1951) <u>A Documentary History of the Negro People in the United States</u>. New York: Citadel Press.

Aptheker, H. (1968) <u>To Be Free</u>. New York: International Publishers.

Asante, M. & Mattson, M. (1991) <u>Historical and Cultural Atlas of African Americans</u>. New York: Macmillan Publishing Co.

Bennett, L. (1988) <u>Before the Mayflower</u>. New York: Penguin Books.

Bennett, L. (1975) <u>The Shaping of Black America.</u> Chicago: Johnson Publishing Co.

Franklin, J. (1988) <u>From Slavery to Freedom: A History of Negro Americans.</u> New York: Alfred A. Knopf.

Karenga, M. (1993) <u>Introduction to Black Studies</u>. Los Angeles: The University of Sandore Press.

Litwack, L. & Meier, A. (1988) <u>Black Leaders of the Nineteenth Century</u>. Chicago: University of Illinois Press.

Low, A. & Clift, V. (eds.) (1983) <u>Encyclopedia of Black America.</u> New York: Neal Schuman Publishers.

McIntyre, C. (1992) <u>Criminalizing a Race: Free Blacks During Slavery</u>. Queens, NY: Kayode Publications.

DAVID WALKER

In 1829, David Walker published the first of four articles that he called <u>Walker's Appeal.</u> In it he encouraged all slaves to become free by killing their masters. The South exploded in anger and offered a reward for Walker of $10,000 dead or alive. Laws were passed threatening to hang anyone with <u>Walker's Appeal</u> in their possession. Anti-slavery leaders of both races in the North and South rejected the violence advocated in Walker's publication and forced him to circulate it at his own risk and expense.

David Walker proclaimed to the slaves: "...it is no more harm for you to kill the man who is trying to kill you than it is for you to take a drink of water." Walker hated slavery despite the fact that he was born free as the product of a free mother and slave father. Afraid that his stirring publication meant eminent danger, Walker's wife and friends urged him to flee to Canada, but he refused. Walker said: "I will stand my ground. Somebody must die in this cause. I may be doomed to the stake and the fire or to the scaffold tree, but it is not in me to falter if I can promote the work of emancipation."

Despite the great efforts of both the North and South to stop its publication, <u>Walker's Appeal</u> became one of the most widely read and circulated books ever written by a Black person. David Walker was considered a hero by most abolitionists, who considered his book the boldest attack ever written against slavery.

Although the violent aspects of <u>Walker's Appeal</u> are most emphasized, he also offered Whites an olive branch if they would end slavery: "Treat us like men, and there is no danger but we will all live in peace and happiness together. For we are not like you: hard hearted, unmerciful, and unforgiving. What a happy country this will be if Whites will listen." Walker viewed his publication as a religious document giving Blacks an obligation from God to eradicate the evils of slavery. Walker said: "...answer God Almighty, had you not rather be killed than to be a slave to a

From David Walker's Appeal

Article I

OUR WRETCHEDNESS IN CONSEQUENCE OF SLAVERY

MY BELOVED BRETHREN:-THE INDIANS OF NORTH AND OF SOUTH AMERICA-THE GREEKS-THE IRISH, SUBJECTED UNDER THE KING OF GREAT BRITAIN-THE JEWS, THAT ANCIENT PEOPLE OF THE LORD-THE INHABITANTS OF THE ISLANDS OF THE SEA-IN FINE, ALL THE INHABITANTS OF THE EARTH, (EXCEPT HOWEVER, THE SONS OF AFRICA) ARE CALLED MEN, AND OF COURSE ARE, AND OUGHT TO BE FREE. BUT WE, (COLOURED PEOPLE) AND OUR CHILDREN ARE BRUTES!! AND OF COURSE ARE, AND OUGHT TO BE SLAVES TO THE AMERICAN PEOPLE AND THEIR CHILDREN FOREVER!! TO DIG THEIR MINES AND WORK THEIR FARMS; AND THUS GO ON ENRICHING THEM, FROM ONE GENERATION TO ANOTHER WITH OUR BLOOD AND OUR TEARS!!!!

I   PROMISED IN A PRECEDING PAGE TO DEMONSTRATE TO THE SATISFACTION OF THE MOST INCREDULOUS, THAT WE, (COLOURED PEOPLE OF THESE UNITED STATES OF AMERICA) ARE THE MOST WRETCHED, DEGRADED AND ABJECT SET OF BEINGS THAT EVER LIVED SINCE THE WORLD BEGAN, AND THAT THE WHITE AMERICANS HAVING REDUCED US TO THE WRETCHED STATE OF SLAVERY, TREAT US IN THAT CONDITION MORE CRUEL (THEY BEING AN ENLIGHTENED AND CHRISTIAN PEOPLE,) THAN ANY HEATHEN NATION DID ANY PEOPLE WHOM IT HAD REDUCED TO OUR CONDITION.

THESE AFFIRMATIONS ARE SO WELL CONFIRMED IN THE MINDS OF ALL UNPREJUDICED MEN, WHO HAVE TAKEN THE TROUBLE TO READ HISTORIES, THAT THEY NEED NO ELUCIDATION FROM ME. BUT TO PUT THEM BEYOND ALL DOUBT, I REFER YOU IN THE FIRST PLACE TO THE CHILDREN OF [OLD TESTAMENT HEBREW PATRIARCH] JACOB, OR OF ISRAEL IN EGYPT, UNDER [EGYPTIAN KING] PHARAOH AND HIS PEOPLE. SOME OF MY BRETHREN DO NOT KNOW WHO PHARAOH AND THE EGYPTIANS WERE-I KNOW IT TO BE A   FACT, THAT SOME OF THEM TAKE THE EGYPTIANS TO HAVE BEEN A GANG OF DEVILS, NOT KNOWING ANY BETTER, AND THAT THEY (EGYPTIANS) HAVING GOT POSSESSION OF

THE LORD'S PEOPLE, TREATED THEM NEARLY AS CRUEL AS CHRISTIAN AMERICANS DO US, AT THE PRESENT DAY. FOR THE INFORMATION OF SUCH, I WOULD ONLY MENTION THAT THE EGYPTIANS, WERE AFRICANS OR COLOURED PEOPLE, SUCH AS WE ARE-SOME OF THEM YELLOW AND OTHERS DARK-A MIXTURE OF ETHIOPIANS AND THE NATIVES OF EGYPT-ABOUT THE SAME AS YOU SEE THE COLOURED PEOPLE OF THE UNITED STATES AT THE PRESENT DAY.-I SAY, I CALL YOUR ATTENTION THEN, TO THE CHILDREN OF JACOB, WHILE I POINT OUT PARTICULARLY TO YOU HIS SON JOSEPH, AMONG THE REST, IN EGYPT........

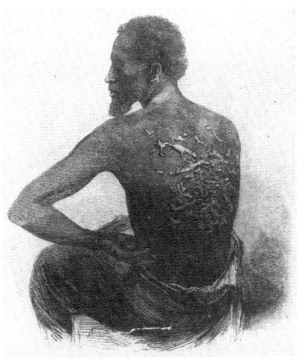

Slave showing back scars

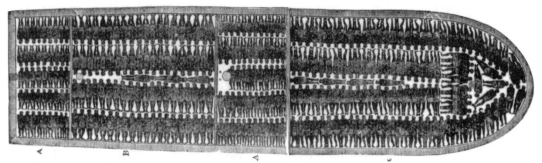

Slave ship below deck

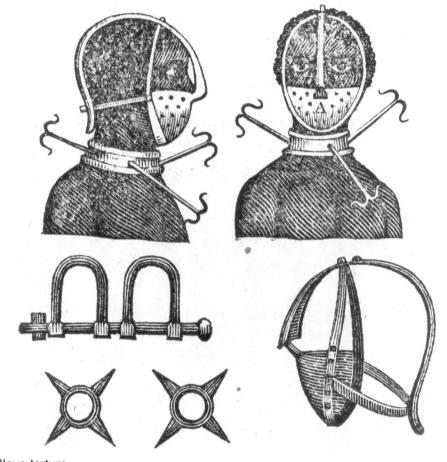

Slave torture

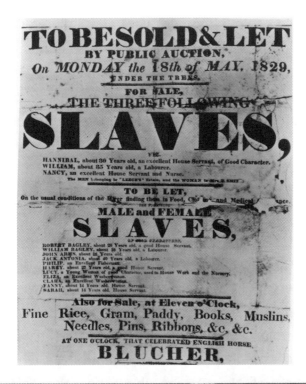

Slave auction

tyrant who takes the life of your mother, wife, and children?" He told the White slaveholders: "You may do your best to keep us in wretchedness and misery to enrich you and your children, but God will deliver us from under you."

David Walker was born in Wilmington, North Carolina, on September 28, 1785. He was self-taught and read extensively the literature on slavery -especially on the history of resistance and oppression. In 1820, he moved to Boston, Massachusetts where he opened a secondhand clothing store. He began writing for a Black newspaper called "The Freedom Journal" in 1827.

David Walker published Walker's Appeal on September 28, 1829. The full title is Walker's Appeal in Four Articles: Together with a Preamble, to the Coloured Citizens of the World, but in Particular, and Very Expressly, to Those of the United States of America. Walker created such fear among slaveholding states that governors and city officials alike held emergency meetings to deal with its obvious implications. True to his word, Walker did not flee the country and was murdered in 1830. The "Appeal" was the inspiration for several slave rebellions including the terrifying slave rebellion of Nat Turner about one year after Walker's death.

David Walker's selfless devotion to the liberation of his people and his revolutionary spirit also served as an important model for future militants like Henry Highland Garnet who published Walker's Appeal and his own work entitled Address to the Slaves of the United States in a single volume in 1848.

REFERENCES AND ADDITIONAL READING

Adams, R. (1969) Great Negroes: Past and Present. Chicago: Afro-Am Publishing Co. Inc.

Al-Mansour, K. (1993) Betrayal by Any Other Name. San Francisco: The First African Arabian Press.

Appiah, K. & Gates, H. (eds.) (1999) Africana. New York: Basis Civitas Books.

Aptheker, H. (1951) A Documentary History of the Negro People in the United States. New York: Citadel Press.

Aptheker, H. (1968) To Be Free. New York: International Publishers.

Bennett, L. (1988) Before the Mayflower. New York: Penguin Books.

Bennett, L. (1975) The Shaping of Black America. Chicago: Johnson Publishing Co.

Franklin, J. (1988) From Slavery to Freedom: A History of Negro Americans. New York: Alfred A. Knopf.

Litwack, L. & Meier, A. (1988) Black Leaders of the Nineteenth Century. Chicago: University of Illinois Press.

Low, A. & Clift, V. (eds.) (1983) Encyclopedia of Black America. New York: Neal Schuman Publishers.

McIntyre, C. (1992) Criminalizing a Race: Free Blacks During Slavery. Queens, NY: Kayode Publications.

Sally C. (1993) The Black 100. New York: Carol Publishing Group.

Wiltse, C. (ed.) (1965) David Walker's Appeal. New York: Hill & Wang.

Zinn, H. (1980) A People's History of the United States. New York: HarperCollins Publishers.

RICHARD ALLEN AND THE AME CHURCH

The African Methodist Episcopal Church (AME Church) was one of the first Black organizations dedicated to Black self-improvement and Pan-Africanist ideals. The AME Church was also distinguished by its commitment to political agitation, Black education, and social activism. The interest in education initially culminated in the founding of Wilberforce University in 1863, as the first Black College founded by Blacks. Numerous other AME Colleges soon followed. AME pastors were also responsible for numerous lawsuits against public school segregation, which eventually led to the 1954 case: "Brown vs. Board of Education." During the Civil

Bishop Richard Allen

Rights movement, the AME Church was very active, and in addition to a pragmatic gospel, the church addressed the housing, welfare, and unionization issues of new immigrants to northern cities. However, nothing more completely captures the spirit and embodiment of the AME Church than its founder and first bishop, Richard Allen.

Richard Allen was born into slavery in Philadelphia, Pennsylvania on February 14, 1760 and shortly thereafter his entire family was sold by a Philadelphia lawyer, Benjamin Chew, to a Delaware plantation owner, Stokely Sturgis. Although the slave master was unconverted, he allowed Richard Allen to attend Methodist meetings. In addition to their antislavery beliefs, Allen was especially impressed by

114

Bethel African Methodist
Episcopal Church

their emphasis on a simple set of virtues including honesty, modesty, and sobriety, and converted to Methodism at age 17. By age 20, Allen was able to convert his slave master and to convince him that slaveholding was wrong. Allen was allowed to buy his freedom for $2,000 by working a variety of odd jobs over the next five years. Once freed, "Allen traveled widely on the Methodist circuits, preaching, holding prayer meetings, and giving religious counsel to groups of White and Black Christians in the small towns and rural settlements of Maryland, Delaware, Pennsylvania, and New York." While in Philadelphia, Allen was asked by the elders at St. George Methodist Church to preach to their Black members. After the Black membership increased dramatically, Richard Allen determined that his calling was to minister to the "uneducated, poor, and unchurched community" and that he could best reach them in a separate Black church. However, the White Methodist elders ridiculed the whole idea with "very degrading and insulting language."

St. George's Black membership became so large that the church was forced to build a new seating gallery. When church authorities demanded that Blacks sit in the rear of the gallery, Allen and others decided they had been insulted enough: "We all went out of the church in a body and they were no more plagued with us." The Black Methodists agreed to purchase a blacksmith shop and to move it to a lot Allen had purchased with his own savings. Carpenters were hired to make the building suitable for church meetings and on April 9, 1794, Bishop Asbury dedicated the structure as "Bethel African Church". Bishop Asbury also ordained Allen as the first Black Methodist deacon and within four years the Bethel membership increased from 45 to 457 members. Richard Allen's success was the inspiration for many other Black Methodist groups to form African Methodist Churches throughout the Northeast, especially in New York, Delaware, and Maryland.

Since Bethel African Church was still under White Methodist ecclesiastical jurisdiction, White Methodists sued for legal control of Bethel, but in 1807, the Pennsylvania Supreme Court ruled in Allen's favor. In 1816, Allen organized a national convention of Black Methodists, since many of them had similar White Methodist challenges. The convention delegates resolved that the churches they represent "should become one body under the name 'African Methodist Episcopal Church' in order to secure their privileges and promote union and harmony among themselves." Richard Allen became the new denomination's first Bishop and retained that title until his death in 1831.

Richard Allen dedicated his entire life toward uplifting his fellow African Americans. He felt that true Christians had to stretch out their hands beyond the circle of family and friends "to comfort the poor neighbor, the stranger, the widow, and the orphan." He helped establish the Free African Society, the Bethel Benevolent Society, and the African Society for the Education of Youth "in order to support one another...from a love to the people of our complexion whom we behold with sorrow." Bethel Church became the scene of numerous Black conventions to discuss the abolition of slavery and racial discrimination, and Richard Allen was commonly recognized as the leader of free Northern Blacks. Allen also published <u>An Address to Those Who Keep Slaves</u> in which he attacked slavery and the arguments for it.

Allen spent the final years of his life vehemently opposing the American Colonization Society, which Whites organized in 1817 to support the emigration of free Blacks from America to Africa. The American Colonization Society argued that free Blacks would have to leave this country to find true freedom, since the Fugitive Slave Act allowed any White person to call a free Black a fugitive slave. Since African Americans could not testify in court and therefore could not defend themselves, they had to find someone White who could speak on their behalf or they would become enslaved. Richard Allen himself was once called a fugitive slave, but fortunately, he was so famous that he not only won his case but had his accuser thrown into jail for three months. The American Colonization Society also argued that African Americans could help civilize and convert their less fortunate African brothers. However, Allen angrily responded that American Blacks could not convert or civilize anyone since they were mostly illiterate and uneducated themselves. He felt the real purpose of the colonizationists was to expel the most vociferous opponents of slavery. Allen told the American Colonization Society: "We will never separate ourselves voluntarily from the slave population in this country; they are our brethren and we feel there is more virtue in suffering privations with them than fancied advantage for a season."

Richard Allen propelled the AME Church to the center of Black institutional activity during his lifetime. Allen's life, as much as his sermons, remained an effective example for the future leadership of the AME Church. Moreover, his leadership direction is responsible for the continued proliferation of AME membership throughout the 19th and 20th centuries, which today boasts a total of over 1.2 million members.

REFERENCES AND ADDITIONAL READING

Adams, R. (1969) <u>Great Negroes: Past and Present</u>. Chicago: Afro-Am Publishing Co. Inc.

Appiah, K. & Gates, H. (eds.) (1999) <u>Africana.</u> New York: Basis Civitas Books.

Aptheker, H. (1951) <u>A Documentary History of the Negro People in the United States.</u> New York: Citadel Press.

Asante, M. & Mattson, M. (1991) <u>Historical and Cultural Atlas of African Americans</u>. New York: Macmillan Publishing Co.

Bennett, L. (1988) <u>Before the Mayflower</u>. New York: Penguin Books.

Bennett, L. (1975) <u>The Shaping of Black America.</u> Chicago: Johnson Publishing Co.

Franklin, J. (1988) <u>From Slavery to Freedom: A History of Negro Americans</u>. New York: Alfred A. Knopf.

Handy, J. (1902) <u>Scraps of African Methodist Episcopal History</u>. Philadelphia: A.M.E. Book Concern.

Litwack, L. & Meier, A. (1988) <u>Black Leaders of the Nineteenth Century</u>. Chicago: University of Illinois Press.

Low, A. & Clift, V. (eds.) (1983) <u>Encyclopedia of Black America</u>. New York: Neal Schuman Publishers.

McIntyre, C. (1992) <u>Criminalizing a Race: Free Blacks During Slavery</u>. Queens, NY: Kayode Publications.

Sally C. (1993) <u>The Black 100</u>. New York: Carol Publishing Group.

Wesley, C. (1935) <u>Richard Allen: Apostle of Freedom.</u> Washington, D.C.

WAR OF 1812

New Orleans monument of Andrew Jackson

African American soldiers and sailors played a tremendous role in helping America defeat the British during the Revolutionary War. Most northern states were so grateful for the contributions of Black soldiers that they abolished slavery shortly after the war. Even Virginia passed a law freeing all slaves who had participated in the Revolutionary War. However, peacetime produced a total amnesia to the contributions of Blacks in the military and a request for their participation was not made again until the War of 1812 (June 18, 1812-December 24, 1814).

After the Revolutionary War, Southerners were determined to never again allow African Americans, neither free nor slave, to "gain dignity and prestige by fighting for the United States." They were instrumental in the passage by Congress of the Military Act (May 8, 1792) which called for the enrollment of "each and every able-bodied White male citizen between the ages of 18 and 45." When the Marine Corps was established by a congressional act on July 11, 1798, Secretary of War Henry Knox issued a directive that "No Negro, mulatto, or Indian is to be enlisted," and this directive was followed for the next 150 years. Only World War II manpower shortages forced the Marine Corps to change its 150-year policy and recruit African Americans. Secretary of the Navy Benjamin Stoddert followed the lead of the Army and Marine Corps and instructed his recruiters in August 1798, "...no Negroes, mulattos, or Indians."

During the early 1800s, the British had the most powerful Navy in the world, especially after defeating France's Napoleonic Navy. Still at war with Napoleon, a British naval blockade from Maine to Georgia was used to prevent American trading with French merchants. Moreover, because of a tremendous shortage of sailors, the British not only boarded and searched merchant vessels on the high seas, but would frequently claim that American sailors were British deserters and force them to work on British ships (called impressments).

The impressments of three African American sailors from the American frigate "Chesapeake" on June 22, 1807, is called the first major incident leading to the War of 1812, and is frequently compared to the killing of Crispus Attucks, which was called the first major incident leading to the Revolutionary War.

Commodores Chancey and Perry praised their Black crew members as among their very best.

A group of expansionist congressmen called "War Hawks" convinced President James Madison to sign a declaration of war against Great Britain on June 18, 1812. In addition to conquering the British on the high seas, they hoped to expel the British from Canada, since most British troops were still fighting Napoleon. However, extreme racism left America ill prepared for this unpopular war. Not only did White men fail to enlist, but New England Whites also started a separatist movement and held a convention in Hartford, Connecticut, in December 1814, to further solidify their demands. Moreover, the Canadian invasion was a total failure, and the British continued to defeat American Whites until they occupied Detroit and most of Ohio. J.A. Rogers states that the British practically wiped out American sea-borne trade and captured Florida, and much of the South, with Black volunteers whom they promised freedom. On August 24, 1814, the British Army captured Washington, D.C. and burned many public buildings to the ground, including the White House and Capital. The Encyclopedia Britannica says America was thoroughly defeated in this war while gaining none of the avowed aims and that only legend has converted defeat into the illusion of victory. Military historian Gary Donaldson states that only after the United States was brought to the edge of losing its independence were African Americans allowed in the military.

White residents of both Pennsylvania and New York now welcomed Blacks into the military to defend their cities from the advancing enemy and even promised slaves freedom after three years of service. General Andrew Jackson begged Blacks in New Orleans to fight the British and promised them equal pay with Whites, 160 acres of land, and participation in all Black battalions led by Black officers to avoid White prejudices. Jackson said: "Through a mistake in policy, you have heretofore been deprived of participation in the glorious struggle for national rights in which our country is engaged. This no longer shall exist. As Americans, your country looks with confidence to her adopted children for a valorous support."

The "Louisiana Battalion of Free Men of Color" were in the front line of American soldiers who severely defeated the British

On March 3, 1813 the Navy officially authorized the recruitment of Blacks because of the severe manpower shortage, thus reversing their official exclusion since the congressional act of 1798. Experienced Black sailors who had previously worked on whaling boats and as merchant marines flocked to the Navy and were credited with much of America's success in defeating the British Navy in the Great Lakes region. Commodore Thomas McDonough said the accuracy of his Black gunners was responsible for his victory on Lake Champlain. Commodore Isaac Chancey said he had fifty Black crew members that were among his very best.

On September 10, 1813, Commodore Oliver Perry defeated the British fleet on Lake Erie after a savage three hour battle and acknowledged the contributions and individual bravery of his 100 Black seamen in his Battle Report and also noted: "They seemed to be absolutely insensitive to danger." Military historian Michael Lanning states: "The American naval victories in which Black sailors played such a critical role, finally forced the war-weary British to agree to a peace treaty." The "Treaty of Ghent" was signed on December 24, 1814, in Belgium, restoring pre-war conditions.

Unaware that the war had ended, sixty British ships containing 12,000 men sailed up the Mississippi River on January 8, 1815, in an attempt to capture New Orleans. The men of the "Louisiana Battalion of Free Men of Color" were in the front line of American soldiers who dealt the British their worst defeat of the war, inflicting 4,000 casualties compared to only sixty of their own. After the battle, General Andrew Jackson praised the Black soldiers: "I was not ignorant that you possessed qualities most formidable to an invading enemy...the President of the United States shall hear how praise worthy was your conduct in the hour of danger." Jackson kept his promises of $124 and 160 acres of land to both White and Black soldiers. However, glory faded quickly for the "Louisiana Battalion of Free Men of Color"; they were soon disbanded and again faced pre-war prejudices. In city celebrations of the "Battle of New Orleans" for the next 100 years, not a single Black person was allowed to participate in the festivities.

White America, again, quickly forgot the contributions of Blacks in the military. A War Department memorandum on March 3, 1815, discharged all Blacks from the military stating: "A Negro is deemed unfit to associate with the American soldier." The Navy issued orders in 1839, restricting Black enlistments to less than 5% and only in positions of cooks, mess boys, and servants, and this was signed by the same Isaac Chauncey who had highly praised his Black sailors during the War of 1812. Peacetime again became the chief promoter of racial exclusion in America and as always, when African Americans were no longer needed, they were also no longer wanted.

REFERENCES AND ADDITIONAL READING

Donaldson, G. (1991) <u>The History of African-Americans in the Military</u>. Malabar, FL: Krieger Publishing Co.

Foner, J. (1974) <u>Blacks and the Military in American History</u>. New York: A New Perspective Publishing Co.

Greene, R. (1974) <u>Black Defenders of America: 1775-1973</u>. Chicago: Johnson Publishing.

Langley, H. (1967) <u>Social Reforms in the United States Navy: 1798-1862</u>. Urbana, IL: University of Illinois Press.

Lanning, M. (1997) <u>The African-American Soldier From Crispus Attucks to Colin Powell.</u> Secaucus, NJ: Carol Publishing Group.

McConnell, R. (1968) <u>Negro Troops of Antebellum Louisiana: A History of the Free Men of Color.</u> Baton Rouge, LA: Louisiana State University Press.

Moebs, T. (1994) <u>Black Soldiers-Black Sailors-Black Ink: Research Guide on African - Americans in U.S. Military History</u>. Chesapeake Bay, MD: Moebs Publishing Co.

Mullen, R. (1973) <u>Blacks in America's Wars</u>. New York: Pathfinder.

Nalty, B. (1986) <u>Strength for the Fight: A History of Black Americans in the Military</u>. New York: Free Press.

Rogers, J. (1989) <u>Africa's Gift to America</u>. St. Petersburg, FL: Helga Rogers Publishing.

Wilson, J. (1977) <u>The Black Phalanx: A History of the Negro Soldier of the United States in the Wars of 1775-1812, 1861-1865</u>. New York: Arno Press.

Zinn, H. (1980) A <u>People's History of the United States</u>. New York: HarperCollins Publishers.

THE JOHN BROWN TEST

Dr. Leonard Jeffries recommends that before you call a White person a "true friend", that person should pass the "John Brown Test". Since history records numerous John Browns, the question is, exactly which John Brown does Dr. Jeffries consider a good role model for White friendship? Rhode Island College changed its name to Brown University in 1804, to honor one person named John Brown. However, this John Brown made his fortune exchanging rum for slaves, so he could not possibly be the White friend role model. John Robert Brown (1909-1993) was Chief Justice for the Fifth Circuit Court of Appeals and played a pivotal role in championing and enforcing civil rights legislation in the South. He is most noted for ordering, in 1962, that African-American James Meredith be enrolled in the all-White University of Mississippi. Most Black people would be happy to have a White friend like John Robert Brown, but Leonard Jeffries says the "real" John Brown died at Harper's Ferry, West Virginia in 1859.

The "real" John Brown had an entire book written about him in 1909, by W.E. Burghardt DuBois, which was most recently reprinted in 1996, by International Publishers. One of the greatest women in African American history, Harriet Tubman, regarded this John Brown and not President Abraham Lincoln, as the true emancipator of her people. The "real" John Brown was born in Torrington, Connecticut on May 9, 1800, about four months before the attempted insurrection of slaves under Gabriel in Virginia, in September of the same year. He was raised in Hudson, Ohio, where his family migrated in 1805. By the age of 16, he had already joined the church and soon became such an experienced bible student that "when any person was reading he would correct the least mistake." His love for religion was exceeded only by his love for family where he fathered 20 well-disciplined, hard-working children. After seven of his children died before adulthood, he concluded that in some way his own sin and shortcomings were bringing upon him

John Brown was a radical abolitionist who often opposed slavery with violence.

"the vengeful punishment of God." He felt his greatest sin was not doing enough "to increase the amount of human happiness."

In 1839, a turning point occurred in Brown's life when he was visited by a Black preacher named Fayette. Fayette described slavery as "the foulest and filthiest blot on 19th century civilization." He added: "as a school of brutality and human suffering, of female prostitution and male debauchery; as a mockery of marriage and defilement of family life; as a darkening of reason, and spiritual death, slavery has no parallel." John Brown fell to his knees and "implored God's blessing on his purpose to make active war on slavery, and he bound his family in solemn and secret compact to labor for emancipation."

John Brown was convinced that the first step toward emancipation was education. He noted that all pro-slavery states were vehemently opposed to educating slaves and made this a capital offense. John was also aware that slaveholders actively pursued African American schools and churches and burned them to the ground after Nate Turner's slave revolt on August 21, 1831. Brown felt that once the master-slave relationship was broken, Black people deserved their own state and educated Blacks would be needed for self-government. He actively campaigned for the establishment of African American schools and even tried to establish a school himself in Hudson, Ohio. When Oberlin College opened its doors to "Negroes" in 1839, and appointed his father as a trustee, John Brown was overjoyed.

On August 1, 1846, Gerrit Smith, a wealthy New York abolition leader, offered free Blacks 100,000 acres of his land in North Elba, New York for farms. Because of the bleak climate and harsh soil, Black farmers found it very difficult to succeed until John Brown volunteered to help. He went to Gerrit Smith at Petersboro, New York in April 1848 and said: "I am something of a pioneer...I will take one of your farms myself, clean it up and plant it, and show my Colored neighbors how such work should be done. I will look after them in all needful ways and be a kind of father to them."

In 1854, the government announced that Kansas would become a slave-free state open for settlement. Consequently, five of Brown's sons moved to Kansas in October 1854 but were appalled at what they discovered. Large pro-slavery gangs were traveling throughout Kansas killing anti-slavery farmers and burning their properties. When John Brown's sons informed him what was happening, he loaded a wagon full of weapons and headed for Kansas. In May 1856, shortly after John Brown's arrival in Kansas, two thousand pro-slavery Missourians surrounded Lawrence, Kansas, the capital city, and brutally killed many of the anti-slavery settlers and sacked and burned half the town. On the same day, Brooks nearly killed Senator Charles Sumner with a crushing blow to the head in the U.S. Senate Chamber for telling the truth about Kansas. John Brown was angry and "indignant that there had been no resistance; that Lawrence was not defended; and denounced the men as trembling cowards, or worse." In retaliation, Brown and his sons entered Missouri at night and dragged five of the pro-slavery ringleaders out of their cabins and hacked them to death with swords. This blow, called the Pottawatomie murders, is said to have freed Kansas by plunging it into civil war, and compelling men to fight for freedom, which they had vainly hoped to gain by political diplomacy. Kansas's anti-slavery settlers repelled Missouri's pro-slavery settlers' last invasion on September 15, 1856, and Kansas was finally declared a slave-free state. John Brown was now free to return to the East to resume his plan to free Southern slaves by force.

Between 1857 and 1859, John Brown visited the homes of Frederick Douglas, Harriet Tubman, Henry Highland Garnet, Martin Delaney, and many other leading African American abolitionists to gain their support for his plan to free all Southern slaves by force. All of the abolitionists were extremely impressed by John Brown's intense desire to end slavery. Although they believed in John Brown, most did not believe his plan was humanly possible. Nevertheless, only sickness prevented Harriet Tubman from joining John Brown on his Southern invasion after she had actively recruited soldiers for his cause.

When told that he might die executing his plan, Brown exclaimed: "Did not my Master Jesus Christ come down from Heaven and sacrifice Himself upon the altar for the salvation of the race, and should I, a worm, not worthy to crawl under his feet, refuse to sacrifice myself?" On October 16, 1859, John Brown with an armed band of 16 Whites (including two of his sons) and five Blacks attacked the federal armory at Harper's Ferry, West Virginia. He had hoped that by capturing the armory arsenal, escaped slaves would join his rebellion, forming an "army of emancipation" with which to liberate their fellow slaves. Unfortunately, he was surrounded by U.S. Marines and overpowered. He was tried and convicted of slave insurrection and hanged on December 2, 1859. Many believe that Brown's attack helped immortalize him and hasten the Civil War, which did bring emancipation.

The last moments of John Brown

If Leonard Jeffries could find a single friend Black or White who even comes close to passing the "John Brown Test", he should consider himself truly blessed. The truth is, only one person in this country's history either Black or White has ever passed the "John Brown Test", and he was the "REAL" John Brown.

REFERENCES AND ADDITIONAL READING

Aaron, D. (1973) <u>The Unwritten War</u>. New York: Oxford University Press.

Appiah, K. & Gates, H. (eds.) (1999) <u>Africana</u>. New York: Basis Civitas Books.

Aptheker, H. (1951) <u>A Documentary History of the Negro People in the United States.</u> New York: Citadel Press.

Aptheker, H. (1969) <u>American Negro Slave Revolts.</u> New York: International Publishers.

Asante, M. & Mattson, M. (eds.) <u>1991 Historical and Cultural Atlas of African Americans.</u> New York: Macmillan Publishing Co.

Bennett, L. (1988) <u>Before the Mayflower</u>. New York: Penguin Books.

DuBois, W. (1972) <u>John Brown</u>. New York: International Publishers.

Franklin, J. (1988) <u>From Slavery to Freedom: A History of Negro Americans.</u> New York: Alfred A. Knopf.

Loewen, J. (1995) <u>Lies My Teacher Told Me.</u> New York: Simon & Schuster.

Low, A. & Clift, V. (eds.) (1983) <u>Encyclopedia of Black America</u>. New York: Neal Schuman Publishers.

Oates, S. (1970) <u>To Purge This Land With Blood</u>. New York: Harper & Row.

Scheidenhelm, R. (ed.) (1972) <u>The Response to John Brown.</u> Belmont, CA: Wadsworth.

Stavis, B. (1970) <u>John Brown: The Sword and the Word</u>. New York: A.S. Barnes.

Warch, R. & Fanton, J. (eds.) <u>John Brown</u>. Englewood Cliffs, NJ: Prentice-Hall.

Zinn, H. (1980) <u>A People's History of the United States</u>. New York: HarperCollins Publishers.

BLACK PEOPLE IN THE OLD WEST

President Roosevelt called December 7, 1941, the day Pearl Harbor was bombed, as a day that will forever be recorded in infamy. For Black pioneers in the old west, February 2, 1848, will forever be recorded in infamy. This is the day the peace treaty was signed which ended the Mexican War and gave to the United States the territories of Texas, California, Nevada, Utah, and parts of Arizona, Wyoming, Colorado, and New Mexico.

The African Americans who arrived with the earliest Spanish expeditions to California helped create a culture that accepted them as equals. Blacks purchased large segments of land and became successful businessmen with the establishment of hotels and trading centers. Los Angeles was founded by 26 people of African ancestry and only two Caucasians. Maria Rita Valdez, whose Black grandparents were among the founding members of Los Angeles, owned Rancho Rodeo de Las Aguas, today called Beverly Hills. Francisco Reyes, another Black resident, owned the San Fernando Valley. In the 1790's, he sold it and became mayor of Los Angeles. Pio Pico, whose grandmother was listed as mulatto in the 1790 census, was governor of California from 1845-1846, when the Mexican War started. Pico Boulevard in Los Angeles and Pico Rivera, CA are named after this Black governor.

Mexican-American War: Battle of Resaca De La Palma

William Leidesdorff is one of San Francisco's most famous citizens. He was born in St. Croix, Virgin Islands to a Danish planter and his African wife. He sailed for California in 1841, after becoming a wealthy businessman, aboard his 160-ton schooner called "Julia Ann." He shortly thereafter became a landowner, having purchased a 35,000-acre estate in San Francisco and soon became treasurer of the San Francisco City Council. He helped set up the first public school system which was open to everyone, regardless of

William Leidesdorf helped set up the first public school system in San Francisco, which was open to everyone.

race, creed, or color. Leidesdorff opened the first hotel in San Francisco, introduced the first steamboat to the city, and organized its first horse race. Today a street in downtown San Francisco bears the name of this remarkable early Black citizen.

Things changed rapidly after February 2, 1948, when the United States assumed control of California. President Polk announced the discovery of gold in California, in 1849, and the population soared ten fold within two years. Although racial lines had been ignored before California became American territory, Black hatred and discrimination moved westward with the White wagon trains. Most White Californians were convinced that no matter how honest, reliable, hard working, or wealthy a Black neighbor might be, he ought not be granted any rights a White man was bound to respect. In 1852, the legislature of California passed a law, deeply hated by Blacks, which prohibited any Black person from testifying in court. This prevented Black men from supporting their land claims, Black women from identifying rape assailants, and Black businessmen from suing those who had cheated or robbed them. Other anti–Black laws produced segregated schools and prohibited Blacks from voting as well as from serving in the military.

In addition, the "fugitive slave law" was passed in 1852, by a 14 to 9 vote, which also permitted a slave owner to remain an indefinite time in the state, thus institutionalizing slavery despite its prohibition in the state constitution.

A Black exodus from California to Canada occurred in 1858, when the California legislature tried to pass a bill banning Black immigration. Blacks were terrified because Oregon's legislature passed a law the previous year, which provided for the expulsion of all Black people within three years. Any Black remaining after three years would be whipped every six months or forced into labor without pay. Oregon's exclusion provision was passed in 1857, and was not repealed until 1927.

Our Black ancestors in the old west could only dream about how wonderful their lives may have been if the Mexican government had won the war and had not signed the peace treaty on the infamous day of February 2, 1848.

REFERENCES AND ADDITIONAL READING

Appiah, K. & Gates, H. (eds.) (1999).Africana New York: Basis Civitas Books.

Aptheker, H. (1951) A Documentary History of the Negro People in the United States. New York: Citadel Press.

Beasley, D. (1919) The Negro Trail Blazer of California. Los Angeles: Times Mirror Printing and Binding House.

Billington, M. & Hardaway, R. (eds.) (1998) African Americans on the Western Frontier. Niwot, CO: University Press of Colorado.

Graebner, N. (ed.) (1968) Manifest Destiny. Indianapolis: Bobbs-Merrill.

Jay, W. (1849) A Review of the Causes and Consequences of the Mexican War. Boston: B.B. Mussey & Co.

Katz, W. (1992) Black People Who Made the Old West. Trenton, NJ: Africa World Press.

Lapp, R. (1977) Blacks in Gold Rush California. New Haven, Connecticut: Yale University Press.

Pelz, R. (1989) Black Heroes of the Wild West. Seattle: Open Hand Publishers.

Ravage, J. (1997) Black Pioneers: Images of the Black Experience on the North American Frontier. Salt Lake City: The University of Utah Press.

Savage, W. (1976) Blacks in the West. Westport: Greenwood Press.

Schroeder, J. (1973) Mr. Polk's War: American Opposition and Dissent 1846-1848. Madison: University of Wisconsin Press.

Smith, G. & Judah, C. (eds.) (1966) Chronicles of the Gringos: The U.S. Army in the Mexican War 1846-1848. Albuquerque: University of Wisconsin Press.

BLACK WOMEN OF THE OLD WEST

Although our novels and movies are filled with heroes from the old west, African American heroes are virtually never mentioned. Moreover, historians have also contributed to this unjust and unbalanced recording of our glorious western saga by completely ignoring the many accomplishments of Black men and women, despite the fact they were accurately reported in newspapers, government records, military reports, and pioneer memoirs. As members of a double minority, Black women have suffered an even greater historical injustice, although they were an integral part of the western fabric. Nothing more clearly demonstrates the contributions of Black women to the western tradition than the biographies of Biddy Bridget Mason, Clara Brown, and Mary Ellen Pleasant.

Biddy Bridget Mason (1815-1891) was born into slavery and given as a wedding gift to a Mormon couple in Mississippi named Robert and Rebecca Smith. In 1847, at age 32, Biddy Mason was forced to walk from Mississippi to Utah, tending cattle behind her master's 300-wagon caravan. After four years in Salt Lake City, Smith took the group to a new Mormon settlement in San Bernardino, California in search of gold. When Biddy Mason discovered that the California State Constitution made slavery illegal, she had Robert Smith brought into court on a writ of habeas corpus, and the court freed all of Smith's slaves. Now free, Mason and her three daughters (probably fathered by Smith) moved to Los Angeles where they worked and saved enough money to buy a house at 331 Spring Street in downtown Los Angeles.

Knowing what it meant to be oppressed and friendless, Biddy Mason immediately began a philanthropic career by opening her home to the poor, hungry, and homeless. Through hard work, saving, and investing carefully, she was able to purchase large amounts of real estate, including a commercial building, which provided her with enough income to help build schools, hospitals, and churches. Her

Biddy Mason walked from Mississippi to California.

most noted accomplishment was the founding of First African Methodist Episcopal (AME) Church, now the oldest church in Los Angeles, where she also operated a nursery and food pantry. Moreover, her generosity and compassion included personally bringing home cooked meals to men in state prison. In 1988, Mayor Tom Bradley had a tombstone erected at her unmarked gravesite and November 16, 1989 was declared "Biddy Mason Day". In addition, the highlights of her life were displayed on a wall of the Spring Center in downtown Los Angeles, an honor befitting Los Angeles' first Black female property owner and philanthropist.

"Aunt" Clara Brown

Clara Brown (1806-1888) is another who dedicated her life to the betterment of others. She was born as a slave in Virginia and then sold at age three to the Brown family in Logan, Kentucky. At age 35, her master died, and her slave husband, son, and daughter were sold at auction to different owners. After 20 additional years in slavery, she was able to buy her freedom and immediately headed west to St. Louis. At age 55, she agreed to serve as cook and laundress in exchange for free transportation in a caravan headed for the gold mines of Colorado. Clara Brown established a laundry in Central City and as her resources expanded, she opened up her home, which served as a hospital, church, and hotel to the town's less fortunate.

Under her direction, the first Sunday school developed, and moreover, the whole town turned to her during illness because she was such a good nurse. Frequently, she even "grubstaked miners who had no other means of support while they looked for gold in the mountains and was repaid handsomely for her kindness and generosity by those who struck pay dirt." Far and wide, she was known as "Aunt Clara" and as "the Angel of the Rockies".

By the end of the Civil War, Clara Brown had accumulated several Colorado properties and over $10,000 in cash. Since slavery was over, she used her fortune to search for relatives in Virginia and Kentucky and returned with 34 of them including her daughter. She continued her philanthropy among the needy for the rest of her life and also spent large sums of money helping other Blacks come west.

Upon her death at age 82, the Colorado Pioneers Association buried her with honors, and a plaque was placed in the St. James Methodist Church stating that her house was the first home of the church.

Mary Ellen Pleasant (1814-1903), a former slave, moved to San Francisco in 1849, where she opened a successful boarding house, famous for cards, liquor, and beautiful women. She was also a partner of Thomas Bell, cofounder of the first "Bank of California". As a businesswoman, she was called mercurial, cunning, cynical, and calculating, but personally she was softhearted and had a passion for

Mary Ellen Pleasant at 87 years of age

helping the less fortunate who called her "the Angel of the West". She was a leader in California for the protection of abused women and children and helped build and support numerous "safe havens" for them. Mary Ellen Pleasant hated slavery and frequently rode into the rural sections of California to rescue people held in bondage. Because of Pleasant, the entire Black community of San Francisco received a warning from one judge for "the insolent, defiant, and dangerous way that they interfered with those who were arresting slaves." Mary Ellen Pleasant used most of her fortune to aid fugitive slaves. "She fed them, found occupations for them, and financially backed them in numerous small businesses." In 1858, she gave $30,000 to John Brown to help finance his raid at Harper's Ferry,

Virginia. This White abolitionist had hoped to capture the national armory and distribute the weapons to slaves for a massive insurrection. During the Civil War, Pleasant raised money for the Union cause and continued to fight for civil rights. Her tombstone epitaph read: "Mother of Civil Rights in California" and "Friend of John Brown".

Brief biographies of Biddy Bridget Mason, Clara Brown, and Mary Ellen Pleasant serve to illustrate the enormous contributions and accomplishments of Black women in the old west. Era Bell Thompson in <u>American Daughter</u> clearly states the problem: "Black women were an integral part of the western and American tradition. It both impairs their sense of identity and unbalances the historical record to continue to overlook the role of Black women in the development of the American west."

REFERENCES AND ADDITIONAL READING

Billington, M. & Hardaway, R. (eds.) (1998) <u>African Americans on the Western Frontier.</u> Niwot, CO: University Press of Colorado.

Bruyn, K. (1970) <u>Aunt Clara Brown: Story of a Black Pioneer</u>. Boulder, CO: Pruett Publishing Co.

James, E. & James, J. (eds.) (1971) <u>Notable American Women</u>. Cambridge, MA: Belknap Press.

Katz, W. (1992) <u>Black People Who Made the Old West.</u> Trenton, NJ: Africa World Press.

Lerner, G. (1979) <u>The Majority Finds Its Past: Placing Women in History</u>. New York: Oxford University Press.

Myres, S. (1982) <u>Westering Women: The Frontier Experience, 1880-1915</u>. Albuquerque: University of New Mexico Press.

Pelz, R. (1989) <u>Black Heroes of the Wild West</u>. Seattle: Open Hand Publishers.

Ravage, J. (1997) <u>Black Pioneers: mages of the Black Experience on the North American Frontier</u>. Salt Lake City: The University of Utah Press.

Riley, G. (1981) <u>Frontierswomen: The Iowa Experience.</u> Ames: Iowa State University Press.

Savage, W. (1976) <u>Blacks in the West</u>. Westport: Greenwood Press.

Sterling, D. (1984) <u>We Are Your Sisters: Black Women in the Nineteenth Century.</u> New York: W.W. Norton & Co.

Thompson, E. (1986) <u>American Daughter.</u> St. Paul: Minnesota Historical Society.

AFRICAN AMERICANS AND THE CIVIL WAR

In a 1928 biography of Ulysses S. Grant, historian W.E. Woodward disavowed any contributions made by Black Americans in the Civil War. He wrote: "The American Negroes are the only people in the history of the world, that ever became free without any effort of their own...The Civil War was not their business." Woodward dismissed the 200,000 African Americans who served in the war and the 28,000 who died fighting. White historians have always diminished the wartime contributions of African Americans (who have served honorably in every war since this country's inception), but no period seems more blatantly ignored than the Civil War. Freedom for Blacks was the lasting legacy of the Civil War, yet most history textbooks would have us believe that Black slaves sat around playing banjoes and awaiting Yankee soldiers to set them free. Nothing could be further from the truth!

The Civil War began on April 12, 1861, when the Confederate Army attacked Fort Sumter. The North initially thought they would easily crush the South because of their 23,000,000 able-bodied White males verses only about 6,000,000 White males available to the South. The North was so certain of victory that they absolutely refused to allow any Black people (free or slave) to participate. President Lincoln, however, had considerable difficulty in obtaining volunteers. Poor White men refused to fight in a war that they believed would liberate slaves who would take their jobs. They also felt that neither saving the Union nor ending slavery was adequate reason for risking their lives. In July 1862, President Lincoln asked for 300,000 men, but in five weeks less than 30,000 volunteered. On March 1, 1863, Congress passed the nation's first draft bill, the National Conscription Act, which was so unpopular that anti-draft riots broke out in several northern cities. Primarily, recently immigrated poor White males vented their anger against local defenseless African Americans. The New York Times wrote that people of African descent were "literally hunted down like wild beasts and when caught either stoned to death or hung from trees and lamp posts."

In addition to a manpower shortage, General Sherman told President Lincoln that "our men are not good soldiers. They brag but they don't perform." The New York World newspaper reported that "when the Confederate calvary charged at Bull Run the Union soldiers ran in panic, leaving artillery, guns, ammunition, wagons, and equipment behind." Sir William Howard Russell, war correspondent of the London Times wrote: "Such cowardly scandalous behavior on the part of soldiers I should never have considered possible." The North was decisively defeated in its first three major battles at Bull Run, Wilson Creek, and Balls Bluff. Horace Greeley of the New York Tribune wrote Lincoln that "the larger part of the army is a confused mob, entirely demoralized." He further added that Lincoln should "make peace with the rebels at once and on their terms." Conceding victory to the Confederacy, Greeley published that "so short-lived has been the American Union that men who saw its rise may now see its fall."

SACKING A DRUG STORE IN SECOND AVENUE.   HANGING A NEGRO IN CLARKSON STREET

New York riots where Blacks were hunted and murdered.

COME AND JOIN US BROTHERS.

Civil War
recruiting
poster

In July 1862, Lincoln convinced his Cabinet that all was lost unless he could "win over the slaves of the South and have them fight on his side by offering them freedom." Lincoln himself wrote the original draft of the Emancipation Proclamation and called a special Cabinet meeting for its presentation. The Cabinet agreed that the proclamation was their last resort, but Secretary of War Seward asked Lincoln if he could wait for some type of Union victory prior to its release. Otherwise, Seward said: "It will be viewed as the last measure of an exhausted government; a cry for help; the government stretching forth its hands to Ethiopia, instead of Ethiopia stretching forth her hands to the government." The opportunity came with the marginal Federal victory at Antietam Creek in Maryland, on September 17, 1862. One week after the Battle of Antietam, Lincoln released the Emancipation Proclamation, which stated that all slaves in the Confederacy (or

The 54th Massachusetts Regiment leading the assault on Fort Wagner, South Carolina, on July 18, 1863

areas still in rebellion) would be "henceforth and forever free". In addition, this document also permitted for the first time, the recruitment of Black men into the army. As a result of these actions, large numbers of newly emancipated slaves all over the South began joining Federal forces as soldiers and laborers.

When it became clear to the Confederate forces in 1863, that their armies would be facing Black soldiers in the field, they responded with a threat of death to all African Americans and their White commanding officers. These were not idle threats. At Fort Pillow, Tennessee, in April 1864, about 300 Black Federal soldiers were massacred under the direction of Confederate General Nathan Bedford Forrest (who later founded the Ku Klux Klan). The Fort Pillow incident caused Black soldiers to fight more desperately throughout the remainder of the war. They either feared that capture meant certain death, or they intended to exact some revenge for the Fort Pillow atrocities or both.

On June 7, 1863 at Milliken's Bend, Louisiana, the Ninth and Eleventh Louisiana regiment won the Civil War's first significant battle secured by African Americans. Assistant Secretary of War Charles Dana reported that "a Confederate force of three thousand attacked the camp and initially forced the Negro troops to give way, but once reminded that those of their number who were captured were killed, they rallied with great fury and routed the enemy."

Although the Louisiana regiments fought the first major battles by African American soldiers in the Civil War, the Fifty-Fourth Massachusetts regiment gained the most widespread and lasting fame of the war during its assault on Confederate Fort Wagner in South Carolina. Most of the men of the Fifty-Fourth regiment were killed while attacking Fort Wagner, yet Northern politicians, newspapers, and military leaders hailed the Fifty-Fourth as a symbol of the country's greatest example of valor in combat. In 1989, Hollywood honored the Fifty-Fourth regiment in a feature film entitled "Glory" which earned an Oscar nomination for best picture.

Black soldiers participated in virtually every major battle, once they were allowed to join the military, and earned 23 Congressional Medals of Honor. Senior Union commanders including Generals Daniel Ullman and Nathaniel Banks, testified that "the brigades of Negroes behaved magnificently and fought splendidly, and they were far superior in discipline to the White troops and just as brave." On August 15, 1864, in an interview with John T. Mills, Lincoln defended the use of Black troops by stating that if the 200,000 Black soldiers had decided to fight for the Confederacy instead of the Union, he would have been "compelled to abandon the war in three weeks."

In summary, history textbooks should record that African American soldiers fought gallantly during the Civil War to end over 200 years of bondage. The Thirteenth Amendment (freeing all slaves) was only another testimony to the magnificent accomplishments of the Black soldiers on the Civil War's battlefields.

Pictured here are 15 of the 23 Black soldiers who were awarded the Medal of Honor for bravery, the United States military's highest honor.

REFERENCES AND ADDITIONAL READING

Donaldson, G. (1991) The History of African-Americans in the Military. Malabar, FL: Krieger Publishing Co.

Foner, J. (1974) Blacks and the Military in American History. New York: A New Perspective Publishing Co.

Greene, R. (1974) Black Defenders of America: 1775-1973. Chicago: Johnson Publishing.

Langley, H. (1967) Social Reforms in the United States Navy: 1798-1862. Urbana, IL: University of Illinois Press.

Lanning, M. (1997) The African-American Soldier From Crispus Attucks to Colin Powell. Secaucus, NJ: Carol Publishing Group.

McConnell, R. (1968) Negro Troops of Antebellum Louisiana: A History of the Free Men of Color. Baton Rouge, LA: Louisiana State University Press.

Moebs, T. (1994) Black Soldiers-Black Sailors-Black Ink: Research Guide on African - Americans in U.S. Military History. Chesapeake Bay, MD: Moebs Publishing Co.

Mullen, R. (1973) Blacks in America's Wars. New York: Pathfinder.

Nalty, B. (1986) Strength for the Fight: A History of Black Americans in the Military. New York: Free Press.

Rogers, J. (1989) Africa's Gift to America. St. Petersburg, FL: Helga Rogers Publishing.

Wilson, J. (1977) The Black Phalanx: A History of the Negro Soldier of the United States in the Wars of 1775-1812, 1861-1865. New York: Arno Press.

Zinn, H. (1980) A People's History of the United States. New York: HarperCollins Publishers.

BLACK COWBOYS

The deaths of Roy Rogers and Gene Autry saddened us all because many of us grew up watching these fictional cowboys help tame the Old West. However, what is even sadder is that virtually none of us can name a single Black cowboy, either real or fictional. The very word "cowboy" was initially only applied to Black men who took care of cows. Similarly, Black men who worked in the house were called "house boys". Nevertheless, once cowboys became the heroes of western novels and later television, Black people totally disappeared from the Old West.

Joseph G. McCoy created the need for "cowboys" when he established a market and railroad-shipping center at Abilene, Kansas. Before McCoy was able to convince the Union Pacific Railroad to extend its tracks into Abilene, ranchers in Texas had no way to get their cattle to beef hungry Eastern and Midwestern markets. Most of the cattle were merely slaughtered for their hides. It was estimated that over four million cattle grazed in Texas at the end of the Civil War. Once the marketplace for buyers and sellers of cattle was created, cattlemen had only to get their herds from Texas into the Abilene, Kansas cattle trains. The best known trail for delivering these cattle was called the Chisholm Trail. Its main stem ran from the Rio Grande through Austin, Waco, and Fort Worth, Texas, before entering Oklahoma and finally Kansas.

A cattle crew of eleven men usually managed an average herd of 2,500 cattle: the trail boss, eight cowboys, a wrangler, and a cook. Approximately two to four Black cowboys were present on most cattle drives because among them were many of the best riders and ropers in the Midwest. Ironically enough, all cowhands–whether White or Black–soon became known as cowboys, which White Texans strongly resented. The eight cowboys usually rode in pairs with two in the front and rear, and two on each side of the herd. Moreover, the cook was usually a retired Black cowboy and the wrangler was frequently a Black teenager who took care of the horses.

Ab Blocker, one of the most famous of the trail bosses, said he intentionally hired large numbers of Black cowboys because of their outstanding performances during the two-three month long, arduous, and dangerous trail drives. One Black cowboy actually saved his life. All the real cowboys–Black, Brown, Red, and White–shared the same jobs and dangers. They ate the same food and slept in the same area. Cowboys had to be willing to work almost day and night to the point of exhaustion and under the most strenuous conditions. They continuously risked death through drowning (at river crossings) and attacks from wild animals, including wolves and snakes. They also faced illness produced by high winds and freezing thunder storms. This constant threat of danger developed an extreme comradery among cowboys on the trail. In fact, when a Black cowboy became the first person imprisoned in the new Abilene jail, his Black and White cowboy crew immediately broke him out and ran the sheriff out of town. At the end of their long cattle drives, a few Black cowboys remained on northern ranges to become horse breakers, ranch hands, and even sheriffs or outlaws, but most of them drew their pay and rode back to Texas for yet another cattle drive.

Despite the legendary performances of great lawmen like Wyatt Earp and Batt Masterson, Black soldiers, known as the Buffalo Soldiers, were primarily responsible for keeping law and order in the Old West. Their peace keeping missions between cattlemen and farmers (who fought to keep cattle off their crops) were primarily responsible for making expansion of the cattle empire possible. The Buffalo Soldiers were also the primary force that helped stop Indian attacks on cattlemen moving up the Chisholm Trail. The Congressional Act of July 28, 1866, established two Black infantry regiments and two Calvary regiments. All four saw continuous service in the West during the three decades following the Civil War. The Black Calvary fought in almost every part of the West from Mexico to Montana. Both General Miles and General Merritt praised their Black troops as "courageous, skilled, intelligent, and brave in battle."

Buffalo Soldiers

It should not be surprising that Black men were among the best horse riders in the Old West because they were traditionally responsible for the care and maintenance of horses while working as stable boys, trainers, and jockeys. In fact, thirteen of the fourteen jockeys who participated in the first running of the Kentucky Derby were Black. Moreover, from 1875 until 1902, Black jockeys won eleven Kentucky Derby titles. Isaac Murphy-who won the Kentucky Derby in 1884, 1890, and 1891- was recognized as America's finest rider during the last two decades of the 19th century. Forty years passed before Earl Sande tied his record of three Kentucky Derby titles. Black jockeys continued their outstanding performances until racism barred them from the racetracks and replaced them with White jockeys.

In July 1876, the booming new town of Deadwood, South Dakota, decided to have a roping contest to settle once and for all who was the best roping cowboy. Contestants came from miles around to win the $200 prize. A Black cowboy named Nat Love-who subsequently wrote his autobiography-was several minutes faster than his nearest competitor. With the roping contest completed, a dispute soon arose over who was the best marksman. Nat Love also won the subsequent shooting contest by placing all fourteen of his rifle shots in the bull's eye target at 150 yards. In addition to the prize money, Nat Love was given the title "Deadwood Dick" which he carried with "honor" ever after.

Nate Love: "Deadwood Dick"

Bill Pickett is credited with having originated the sport of "bulldogging". Bulldogging is defined as "throwing a steer by seizing the horns and twisting the neck". According to Bill Pickett's boss, Zack Miller, who owned the 101 Ranch, "Bill Pickett was the greatest sweat and dirt cowhand that ever lived–bar none." The Miller Brothers' 101 Ranch later became famous for putting on one of the finest rodeos in the world and played in such places as Chicago, New York, London, and Mexico City. One of their greatest attractions was Bill Pickett who would actually bring down steers with only his teeth.

As the agricultural frontier moved west, the open range was transformed into farms with barbed-wire boundaries, which significantly reduced the public domain for cattle trails. The long cattle drives also gradually declined as the railroads built branch lines into large Texas cities. By 1890, the legendary era of the cowboy was over, except in fictional novels where Black cowboys completely vanished from their role as self-reliant and masterful heroes of the Old West.

REFERENCES AND ADDITIONAL READING

Abbott, E. & Smith, H. (1939) <u>We Pointed Them North: Recollections of a Cowpuncher</u>. New York: Farrar & Rinehart.

Adams, A. (1931) <u>The Log of a Cowboy</u>. Boston: Houghton Mifflin Co.

Adams, R. (ed.) (1957) <u>The Best of the American Cowboy</u>. Norman: University of Oklahoma Press.

Atherton, L. (1961) <u>The Cattle Kings.</u> Bloomington, Indiana: Indiana University Press.

Bard, F. (1960) <u>Horse Wrangler: Sixty Years in the Saddle in Wyoming and Montana.</u> Norman: University of Oklahoma Press.

Billington, M. & Hardaway, R. (eds.) (1998) <u>African Americans on the Western Frontier</u>. Niwot, CO.: University Press of Colorado.

Branch, E. (1961) <u>The Cowboy and His Interpreters</u>. New York: Cooper Square Publishers.

Bronson, E. (1910) <u>Cowboy Life on the Western Plains. The Reminiscences of a Ranchman.</u> New York: George H. Doran Co.

Durham, P. & Jones, E. (1965) <u>The Negro Cowboys</u>. Lincoln: University of Nebraska Press.

Katz, W. (1992) <u>Black People Who Made the Old West.</u> Trenton, NJ: Africa World Press.

Leckie, W. (1967) <u>The Buffalo Soldiers</u>. Norman: University of Oklahoma Press.

Pelz, R. (1989) <u>Black Heroes of the Wild West</u>. Seattle: Open Hand Publishers.

Ravage, J. (1997) <u>Black Pioneers: Images of the Black Experience on the North American Frontier</u>. Salt Lake City: The University of Utah Press.

Savage, W. (1976) <u>Blacks in the West.</u> Westport: Greenwood Press.

THE BLACK STATUE OF LIBERTY

In 1798, Napoleon Bonaparte stated that history was only "a lie agreed upon." Nothing could be more illustrative than the history of the Statue of Liberty, originally called "Liberty Enlightening the World." The liberation of African-American slaves was the only inspiration for the creation of a Statue of Liberation for Edouard Rene LeFebvre DeLaboulaye. He recruited a young sculptor, Frederick Auguste Bartholdi, to create a Black female slave statue holding a broken chain in her left hand and with broken chains of slavery at her feet.

The official web site of the Statue of Liberty states that the statue was given to the people of the United States by the people of France as an expression of friendship and to commemorate the centennial of American Independence (1776). The Encyclopedia Britannica states Bartholdi designed the Statue of Liberty as a monument to the Franco-American alliance of 1778. These are absolute and total lies! Edouard Rene LeFebvre DeLaboulaye, an internationally renowned lawyer and author of a three-volume history of the United States, first discussed the idea of a symbol to represent the end of U.S. slavery at a dinner party in 1865, at his country home near Versailles, France. In attendance at the dinner party were many abolitionists, including Victor Hugo and Frederick Auguste Bartholdi, who had initially been retained to create a sculptured bust of Mr. DeLaboulaye.

Victor Hugo and Edouard DeLaboulaye were leaders of the French abolitionist movement. They hated slavery and were in strong support of John Brown, when he attempted to arm slaves in West Virginia for rebellion by raiding the armory at Harper's Ferry in 1859. After John Brown failed and was hanged, Hugo and DeLaboulaye took up a collection among the French people and presented a gold medal to John Brown's widow.

After Abraham Lincoln was elected President of the United States in 1861, the French liberals and abolitionists including Hugo, Bartholdi, and DeLaboulaye urged

Lincoln to free the slaves, even if civil war resulted. Lincoln was told: "You would become the first country in history to have fought a war against itself to free the internal slave and you would go down in history as a truly great country and a beacon of light to all freedom loving people." The French abolitionists saw the Emancipation Proclamation of 1863 as a worthless piece of paper, since it only freed slaves in the Confederate controlled states where Lincoln had no jurisdiction and not in Union controlled states where Lincoln was still in authority. When the war ended in 1865, French abolitionists were extremely happy and, in addition to again urging Lincoln to free all slaves, DeLaboulaye and Bartholdi requested permission to build and dedicate a monument or colossal statuary to that freeing of all slaves in America. When Abraham Lincoln was assassinated, DeLaboulaye again headed the abolitionists' committee that presented a gold medal to Mrs. Lincoln, just as he had done for the widow of John Brown.

In addition to a staunch abolitionist, Frederic Auguste Bartholdi (1834-1904) was an outstanding French sculptor. Bartholdi trained to be an architect in Alsace and Paris and then studied painting with Ary Scheffer and sculpture with J.F. Soitoux. Bartholdi's life and ideas changed dramatically after 1855, when he toured Egypt and witnessed the magnificent colossal monuments and statues created by the ancient Black Egyptians. Bartholdi's creation of a giant Black ex-slave female with broken chairs at her feet and left hand was readily accepted in France. Although liberals, freemasons, and businessmen with American interests were the most enthusiastic supporters of the project, by 1881, some 100,000 people and 181 towns throughout France had contributed money.

In 1871, Frederic Bartholdi, at the urging of DeLaboulaye undertook a voyage to America to sell his idea of a colossal statue clearly symbolizing the end of chattel slavery in the United States. He was armed with a large terracotta statue and numerous drawings to clearly illustrate his proposed Statue of Liberty. The original model of the Statue of Liberty with the broken chains in her hand and on her feet,

No. 1,551.—Vol. LX.]   NEW YORK—FOR THE WEEK ENDING JUNE 13, 1885.   [Price, 10 Cents.

Frederic Auguste Bartholdi and his Statue of Liberty

and with African facial features is still available for viewing at the Museum of the City of New York that is located at Fifth Avenue and 103rd Street. The original African face of the Statue of Liberty was also published in The New York Post dated June 17, 1986, as part of the centennial celebration. Bartholdi found little American support for his African slave model. In 1878, as the African head of Miss Liberty first went on display at the Universal Exposition in Paris, France, rampant reaction raged throughout the American South.

Statue of Liberty after remodeling

Bartholdi finally had to abandon his original ideas and changed the Statue of Liberty to the features we are now familiar with.   The African face was re-sculptured into the face of his mother, Madame Bartholdi.   A tablet of law tucked into her folded arm that bears the date July 4, 1776, replaced the broken chains in the slave's left hand.   Ironically, the chains were left at the feet but the meaning changed from broken American slavery to broken English tyranny.

On May 18, 1986, during the centennial celebration, The New York Times joined The New York Post in describing the original Statue of Liberty and the intention of DeLaboulaye and Bartholdi in presenting this statue to America.   It's unconscionable that the Encyclopedia Britannica and the official Statue of Liberty literature can still lie and say that this is a monument celebrating American Independence of 1776, and/or the Franco-American alliance of 1778.   Dr. Jack Felder sums it up clearly: "Once in place, Miss Liberty received a new meaning. She was hailed as the 'Mother of White Exiles', greeting European immigrants seeking freedom in America.   Nothing in the original conceptions of Bartholdi or DeLaboulaye envisioned this role for their statue."

REFERENCES AND ADDITIONAL READING

Felder, J. (1992) <u>From the Statue of Liberty to the Statue of Bigotry</u>. New York: Jack Felder.

Felder, J. "This Miss Liberty Was Modeled on Racism." <u>Black American</u>, July 3, 1986.

Felder, J. "Black Origins and Lady Liberty." <u>Daily Challenge</u>, July 16, 1990.

Bohlen, C. "Does She Say the Same Things in her Native Tongue?" <u>New York Times</u>, May 18, 1986.

Robinson, C. & Battle, R. (1987) <u>The Journey of the Songhai People.</u> Philadelphia: Farmer Press.

Sinclair, T. "Was Original Statue A Tribute to Blacks?" <u>New York Voice,</u> July 5, 1986.

"Statue of Liberty." <u>The New York Post</u>, June 17, 1986.

LYNCHING

Lynching is defined as mob execution, usually by hanging, without the benefit of trial and often accompanied with torture and body mutilation. The usual scenario included a mob of up to 5,000 White men attacking a single, defenseless Black man and executing him for a crime he was never convicted of, or even charged with in most cases. Lynching is considered one of the most horrific chapters in African American history and is only exceeded by slavery in cruelty and savagery toward another human being.

Ironically, the term "lynch" is derived from the name of Charles Lynch, a Virginia planter and patriot during the American Revolution, who directed violence toward White British loyalists. After the Civil War and emancipation, lynching

Civilization
in the
United
States in
1930

became almost synonymous with hanging and torturing African American males. Between 1882 and 1930, more than 3,300 Black male victims were hanged, burned alive, castrated, and mutilated by mostly southern White mobs who never faced any charges for these criminal acts. Coroners and law officials typically attributed the murders to "parties unknown". Most historians and sociologists agree that mob executions was really about social control and to maintain the status quo of White superiority and had little to do with crime control.

Ida B. Wells (1862-1931) could easily be called the mother of the anti-lynching movement. She was the first of eight children born to slave parents in Holly Springs, Mississippi. After emancipation, she attended several schools run by northern Methodist missionaries, including Rust College. In 1879, after the yellow fever epidemic claimed the lives of both her parents, she moved to Memphis,

Tennessee, with the younger children and accepted a teaching position. Because of her great concern for racial injustice, Wells was invited to write for a local church paper. As her fame increased, she was asked to contribute to several Baptist newspapers. She eventually became editor and partner of the "Free Speech and Headlight" Baptist newspaper.

In 1892, the brutal lynching of three close friends in Memphis started Ida B. Wells on a militant, uncompromising, single-minded crusade against lynching from which she would never retreat. Her three friends committed the crime of opening a grocery store, which successfully competed with a White grocer directly across the street. For the crime of becoming too "uppity", a large White mob took the three proprietors from their grocery store, tortured and killed them. Ms. Wells wrote angry editorials in her newspaper encouraging Blacks to leave Memphis, if possible, and to boycott White businesses, which left several White companies including the newly opened streetcar line on the verge of bankruptcy.

LYNCHING NUMBERS

Years	White	Black	Total
1882-1891	751	732	1,483
1892-1901	381	1,124	1,505
1902-1911	77	707	784
1912-1921	50	554	604
1922-1931	23	201	224
1932-1941	10	95	105
1942-1951	2	25	27
1952-1961	1	5	6
1962-1968	2	2	4

Ida B. Wells-Barnett

Ida B. Wells decided to launch her anti-lynching movement on several fronts. She first wanted to explode the myth that lynching was primarily to protect White women from rape by Black men. She published detailed statistics on lynching, which demonstrated that less than one-fifth of the victims of lynch mobs were even accused of rape by their killers. She said that racist Southern White mobs "cry rape" to brand their victims as "moral monsters" and to place them "beyond the pale of human sympathy." She wrote that while Southern White men raped Black women and children with impunity, they considered any liaison between a Black man and a White woman as involuntary by definition. She pointed out that children produced by White-Black relationships were called "mulatto" from the Spanish word for mule because racist Whites believed that mixed-race children, like the offspring of donkeys and horses, were an inferior breed that could not reproduce. When Ms. Wells suggested in print that White women were often willing participants with Black men, a large White mob destroyed the presses of her newspaper and would have killed her had she not been visiting friends in New York. Thomas Fortune invited her to stay in New York and write for the "New York Age". She was also allowed to exchange the circulation list of the "Free Speech" for a one fourth interest in the "Age" and immediately began to write a series on lynching.

The second approach of Ida B. Wells in her anti-lynching movement was to appeal to the Christian conscience of powerful non-Southern Whites. She published two pamphlets (Southern Horror in 1892, and A Red Book in 1895) in hopes that extensive statistical analysis of lynching would clearly point out that the Southern rape fantasy was merely "an excuse to get rid of Negroes who were acquiring wealth and property." She pointed out that the same lynch mob that killed a Nashville Black man accused of visiting a White woman left unharmed a White man convicted of raping an eight-year-old girl. Since Ms. Wells viewed lynching as primarily an economic issue, she hoped that economic pressure from the "ruling-class Whites" could produce Southern social change. She began a lecture tour in the Northeast in 1892, and in 1894, she lectured in England, where she helped organize the British Anti-Lynching Society. Ms. Wells was able to effect a curtailment of British investment in the South by suggesting that this could influence American sentiment. In 1895, Ida B. Wells toured the northern and western states organizing American anti-lynching societies.

Ida B. Wells told African Americans that her analysis of mob violence suggested that it abated whenever Blacks exercised "manly self-defense". In Southern Horrors she suggested, "a Winchester rifle should have a place of honor in every Black home." She also told Blacks that they must retaliate with their economic power. She urged Blacks to boycott White businesses or to migrate to Oklahoma since Black labor was the industrial strength of the South. She said: "The more the Afro-American yields and cringes and begs, the more he has to do so, the more he is insulted, outraged, and lynched."

Since Southern courts would not punish lynching participants, Ms. Wells lobbied for legislation that would make lynching a federal crime. In 1901, Ida B. Wells met with President William McKinley and pressed for his support with anti-lynching legislation. However, she could not get McKinley or Theodore Roosevelt to support an anti-lynching bill that was introduced in Congress in 1902.

As one of the founding members of the NAACP in 1909, she made her anti-lynching campaign, including anti-lynching legislation, among the NAACP's highest priorities. The NAACP investigated specific incidents and published national statistics on lynching in an attempt to sway public support to put a stop to lynching. In 1918, the NAACP was able to get Republican Congressman Leonidas Dyer to introduce a bill that subjected lynch mobs to a charge of capital murder for their actions. The Dyer Bill passed in the House of Representatives but failed in the Senate because Southern Democrats never allowed the bill out of committee. Congressman Dyer re-introduced the bill each year for the next ten years, but it never again passed either House.

As a result of the life-long crusade of Ida B. Wells against lynching, she became the inspiration for organizations throughout the country that opposed lynching. For example, The American Civil Liberties Union, The Commission on Interracial Cooperation, and The Communist Party of the United States all played a role in the anti-lynching campaign. Ironically, White middle class Southern women for whom lynching was suppose to protect, formed the Jessie Daniel Ames Association of Southern Women for the Prevention of Lynching in 1930. In honor of her legacy, a low-income housing project in Chicago was named after Ida B. Wells in 1941; and in 1990, the U.S. Postal Service issued an Ida B. Wells commemorative stamp. The "militant", "uncompromising", "outspoken", and "fearless" Ida B. Wells can surely look back upon her life as a genuine success in helping to end one of the most horrific chapters in African American history.

REFERENCES AND ADDITIONAL READING

Adams, R. (1969) <u>Great Negroes: Past and Present</u>. Chicago: Afro-Am Publishing Co., Inc.

Appiah, K. & Gates, H. (eds.) (1999) <u>Africana</u>. New York: Basis Civitas Books.

Aptheker, B. (ed.) (1977) <u>Lynching and Rape: An Exchange of Views.</u> American Institute for Marxist Studies.

Aptheker, H. (1951) <u>A Documentary History of the Negro People in the United States</u>. New York: Citadel Press.

Bennett, L. (1988) <u>Before the Mayflower.</u> New York: Penguin Books.

Bennett, L. (1975) <u>The Shaping of Black America</u>. Chicago: Johnson Publishing Co.

Davis, M. (1982) <u>Contributions of Black Women to America.</u> Columbia, South Carolina: Kenday Press.

Duster, A. (1970) <u>Crusade for Justice: The Autobiography of Ida B. Wells</u>. Chicago: University of Chicago Press.

Franklin, J. (1988) <u>From Slavery to Freedom: A History of Negro Americans.</u> New York: Alfred A. Knopf.

Franklin, J. & Meier, A. (eds.) (1982) <u>Black Leaders of the Twentieth Century</u>. Chicago: University of Illinois Press.

Lerner, G. (ed.) (1973) <u>Black Women in America. A Documentary History</u>. New York: Vintage Books.

Low, A. & Clift, V. (eds.) (1983) <u>Encyclopedia of Black America</u>. New York: Neal Schuman Publishers.

Sally, C. (1993) <u>The Black 100</u>. New York: Carol Publishing Group.

FIVE BLACK PRESIDENTS

Joel A. Rogers and Dr. Auset Bakhufu have both written books documenting that at least five former presidents of the United States had Black people among their ancestors. If one considers the fact that European men far outnumbered European women during the founding of this country, and that the rape and impregnation of an African female slave was not considered a crime, it is even more surprising that these two authors could not document Black ancestors among an ever larger number of former presidents. The presidents they name include Thomas Jefferson, Andrew Jackson, Abraham Lincoln, Warren Harding, and Calvin Coolidge.

The best case for Black ancestry is against Warren G. Harding, our 29th president from 1921 until 1923. Harding himself never denied his ancestry. When Republican leaders called on Harding to deny the "Negro" history, he said, "How should I know whether or not one of my ancestors might have jumped the fence?" William Chancellor, a White professor of economics and politics at Wooster College in Ohio, wrote a book on the Harding family genealogy and identified Black ancestors among both parents of President Harding. Justice Department agents allegedly bought and destroyed all copies of this book. Chancellor also said that Harding's only academic credentials included education at Iberia College, which was founded in order to educate fugitive slaves.

Andrew Jackson was our 7th president from 1829 to 1837. The <u>Virginia Magazine of History</u>, Volume 29, says that Jackson was the son of a White woman from Ireland who had intermarried with a Negro. The magazine also said that his eldest brother had been sold as a slave in Carolina. Joel Rogers says that Andrew Jackson Sr. died long before President Andrew Jackson Jr. was born. He says the president's mother then went to live on the Crawford farm where there were Negro slaves, and that one of these men was Andrew Jr's father. Another account of the

Calvin Coolidge

Andrew Jackson

Warren Harding & Grand-Uncle

Thomas Jefferson

Abraham Lincoln

Abraham Lincoln cartoon nicknaming him "Abraham Africanus the First"

"brother sold into slavery" story can be found in David Coyle's book entitled <u>Ordeal of the Presidency</u> (1960).

Thomas Jefferson was our 3rd president from 1801 to 1809. The chief attack on Jefferson was in a book written by Thomas Hazard in 1867, called <u>The Johnny Cake Papers</u>. Hazard interviewed Paris Gardiner, who said he was present during the 1796, Presidential campaign, when one speaker stated that Thomas Jefferson was "a mean-spirited son of a half-breed Indian squaw and a Virginia mulatto father." In his book entitled <u>The Slave Children of Thomas Jefferson</u>, Samuel Sloan wrote that Jefferson destroyed all of the papers, portraits, and personal effects of his mother, Janc Randolph Jefferson, when she died on March 31, 1776. He even wrote letters to every person who had ever received a letter from his mother, asking them to return that letter. Sloan says, "There is something strange and even

169

psychopathic about the lengths to which Thomas Jefferson went to destroy all remembrances of his mother, while saving over 18,000 copies of his own letters and other documents for posterity."   One must ask, "What is it he was trying to hide?"

Abraham Lincoln was our 16th president from 1861 to 1865. J. A. Rogers quotes Lincoln's mother, Nancy Hanks, as saying that Abraham Lincoln was the illegitimate son of an African man. William Herndon, Lincoln's law partner, said that Lincoln had very dark skin and coarse hair and that his mother was from an Ethiopian tribe. In Herndon's book entitled The Hidden Lincoln he says that Thomas Lincoln could not have been Abraham Lincoln's father because he was sterile from childhood mumps and was later castrated. Lincoln's presidential opponents made cartoon drawings depicting him as a Negro and nicknamed him "Abraham Africanus the First."

Calvin Coolidge was our 30th president, and he succeeded William Harding. He proudly admitted that his mother was dark because of mixed Indian ancestry. However, Dr. Bakhufu says that by 1800, the New England Indian was hardly any longer pure Indian, because they had mixed so often with Blacks. Calvin Coolidge's mother's maiden name was "Moor." In Europe the name "Moor" was given to all Black people just as the name Negro was used in America.

All of the presidents mentioned were able to pass for White and never acknowledged their Black ancestry. Millions of other children who were descendants of former slaves have also been able to pass for White. American society has had so much interracial mixing that books such as The Bell Curve, discussing IQ evaluations based solely on race, are totally unrealistic.

REFERENCES AND ADDITIONAL READING

Adler, D. (1987) <u>Thomas Jefferson: Father of our Democracy.</u> New York: Holiday House.

Bakhufu, A. (1993) <u>The Six Black Presidents.</u> Washington, D.C.: PIK2 Publications.

Bennett, L. (1988) <u>Before the Mayflower</u>. New York: Penguin Books.

Brodie , F. (1974) <u>Thomas Jefferson, An Intimate History</u>. New York: W.W. Norton & Co.

Curtis, J. (1982) <u>Return to These Hills: The Vermont Years of Calvin Coolidge</u>. Woodstock, Vermont: Curtis-Lieberman Books.

Dennis, R. (1970) <u>The Black People of America</u>. New York: McGraw-Hill Book Co.

Erikson, E. (1974) <u>Dimensions of a New Identity: Jefferson Lectures</u>. New York: W.W. Norton & Co.

Kane, J. (1981) <u>Facts About the Presidents: From George Washington to Ronald Reagan</u>. New York: The H.W. Wilson Co.

Mapp, A. (1987) <u>Thomas Jefferson: A Strange Case of Mistaken Identity</u>. New York: Madison Books.

Morrow, E. (1963) <u>Black Man in the White House.</u> New York: Coward-McCann Inc.

Remini, R. (1966) <u>Andrew Jackson</u>. New York: Harper & Row.

Reuter, E. (1969) <u>The Mulatto in the United States.</u> Haskell House.

Rogers, J. (1965) <u>The Five Negro Presidents.</u> St. Petersburg, FL: Helga Rogers Publishing.

Rogers, J. (1970) <u>Sex and Race</u>. St. Petersburg, FL: Helga Rogers Publishing.

Sullivan, M. (1991) <u>Presidential Passions: The Love Affairs of America's Presidents-From Washington and Jefferson to Kennedy and Johnson</u>. New York: Shapolsky Publishers Inc.

Whitney, T. (1975 <u>The Descendants of the Presidents</u>. Charlotte, NC: Delmar Printing Co.

BLACK INVENTORS

When the famous anthropologist, Dr. Richard Leakey discovered bones in Africa in 1956, that were millions of years old, his accomplishment was belittled by people who regularly asked the question, "but what has Africa contributed to world progress?" He could not understand why people were so poorly informed, since he knew that the collective contributions of Black people to civilization, science, and invention are so extensive that it is not possible to live a full day in the United States, or any other part of the world without sharing in the benefits of those contributions. Still the genius of the Black imagination that has influenced every aspect of life in the United States and elsewhere is virtually unknown to most people.

Very few homes in America have as many as two books, which discuss the achievements of the Black race, either past or present. During the slave trade, many of the slaves from the former Songhay Empire were highly educated and were credited with teaching Caribbean and American farmers successful agricultural techniques. They also invented various tools and equipment to lessen the burden of their daily work. Most slave inventors were nameless, such as the slave owned by the Confederate President Jefferson Davis who designed the ship propeller used by the entire Confederate Navy.

Following the Civil War, the growth of industry in this country was tremendous and much of this was made possible with inventions by ethnic minorities. By 1913, over 1,000 inventions were patented by Black Americans. Among the most notable inventors were Jan Matzeliger, who developed the first machine to mass-produce shoes, and Elijah McCoy, who invented automatic lubrication devices for steam engines. Granville Woods had 35 patents to improve electric railway systems, including the first system to allow moving trains to communicate. He even sued Alexander Graham Bell and Thomas Edison for stealing his patents and won both cases. Garrett Morgan developed the first automatic traffic signal and gas mask,

Elijah McCoy

Grandville Woods

Lewis Latimer

Norbert Rillieux

and Norbert Rillieux created the technique for converting sugar cane juice into white sugar crystals.   (Moreover, Rillieux was so brilliant that in 1854 he left Louisiana and went to France where he spent ten years working with the Champollions deciphering Egyptian hieroglyphics from the Rosetta Stone). Lewis Latimer created an inexpensive cotton-thread filament, that made electric light bulbs practical, because Edison's original light bulb only burned for a few minutes.   More recent inventors include McKinley Jones, who invented the movable refrigeration unit that is used for transporting food in trucks and trains, and Lloyd Quarterman who, with six other Black scientists, worked on the creation of the atomic bomb (code named: The Manhattan Project.)   Quarterman also helped in the development of the first nuclear reactor, that was used in the atomically powered submarine called the Nautilus.

Let's conclude with two current contributors.   It should not be surprising that we do not know about the wonderful contributions of Blacks in the past because we are not even made aware of the startling scientific achievements during our own lifetime.   For example, Otis Bodkin invented an electrical device used in all guided missiles and all IBM computers, and Colonel Frederick Gregory, who was not only the first Black astronaut pilot but the person who also redesigned the cockpits for the last three space shuttles.   Gregory was also on the team that pioneered the microwave instrumentation landing system.   In year 2000, Bendix Aircraft Company began a worldwide promotion of this microwave instrumentation landing system that can land planes without a pilot.

PRODUCT	BLACK INVENTOR	DATE
AIR CONDITIONING UNIT	FREDERICK M. JONES	JULY 12, 1949
AUTO CUT-OFF SWITCH	GRANVILLE T. WOODS	JANUARY 1, 1889
AUTO FISHING DEVISE	G. COOK	MAY 30, 1899
AUTOMATIC AIR BRAKE	G. T. WOODS	JUNE 10, 1902
AUTOMATIC GEAR SHIFT	RICHARD SPIKES	DECEMBER 6, 1932
BABY BUGGY	W. H. RICHARDSON	JUNE 18, 1889
BICYCLE FRAME	I. R. JOHNSON	OCTOBER 10, 1899
BISCUIT CUTTER	A. P. ASHBOURNE	NOVEMBER 30,1875
BOTTLE	A. C. RICHARDSON	DECEMBER 12, 1899
BOTTLE CAPS	JONES & LONG	SEPTEMBER 13, 1898
BRIDGE SAFETY GAUGES	H. H. REYNOLDS	OCTOBER 7, 1890
BRIDLE BIT	L. F. BROWN	OCTOBER 25, 1892
CASKET LOWERING DEVICE	A. C. RICHARDSON	NOVEMBER 13, 1894
CELLULAR PHONE	HENRY T. SAMPSON	JULY 6, 1971
CHAMBER COMMODE	T. ELKINS	JANUARY 9, 1872
CISTERN CLEANERS	R. H. GRAY	APRIL 9, 1895
CLOTHES DRYER	G. T. SAMPSON	JUNE 7, 1892
COCONUT OIL REFINING	A. P. ASHBOURNE	JULY 27, 1880
CURTAIN ROD	S. R. SCOTTRON	AUGUST. 30, 1892
CURTAIN ROD SUPPORT	WILLIAM S. GRANT	AUGUST 4, 1896
DOOR STOP	O. DORSEY	DECEMBER 10, 1878
DUST PAN	LAWRENCE P. RAY	AUGUST 3, 1897
EGG BEATER	WILLIE JOHNSON	FEBRUARY 5, 1884
ELECTRIC LAMP	LATIMER & NICHOLS	SEPTEMBER 13, 1881
ELECTRIC RAIL TROLLEY	E. R. ROBINSON	SEPTEMBER 19, 1893
ELEVATOR	ALEXANDER MILES	OCTOBER 11, 1887
EYE PROTECTOR	P. JOHNSON	NOVEMBER 2, 1880

PRODUCT	BLACK INVENTOR	DATE
FIRE ESCAPE LADDER	J. B. WINTERS	MAY 7, 1878
FIRE EXTINGUISHER	T. J. MARSHALL	MAY 26, 1872
FOLDING BED	L. C. BAILEY	JULY 18, 1899
FOUNTAIN PEN	W. B. PURVIS	JANUARY 7, 1890
FURNITURE CASTER	D. A. FISHER	MARCH 14, 1876
GAS BURNER	B. F. JACKSON	APRIL 4, 1899
GAS MASK	GARRETT MORGAN	OCTOBER 13, 1914
GAUGE	E. H. HOLMES	NOVEMBER 12, 1895
GOLF TEE	G. F. GRANT	DECEMBER 12 1899
GUITAR	R. F. FLEMMING, JR.	MARCH 3, 1886
HAIR BRUSH	LYDIA D. NEWMAN	NOVEMBER 15, 1898
HAMMOCK & STRETCHER	C. V. RICHEY	DECEMBER 13, 1893
HAND STAMP	WALTER B. PURVIS	FEBRUARY 27, 1883
HEATING APPARATUS	B. F. JACKSON	MARCH 1, 1898
HORSESHOE	J. RICKS	MARCH 30, 1886
ICE CREAM SCOOPER	A. L. CRALLE	FEBRUARY 2, 1897
INSECT-DESTROYER GUN	A. C. RICHARDSON	FEBRUARY 28, 1899
IRONING BOARD	SARAH BOONE	APRIL 26, 1892
KITCHEN TABLE	H. A. JACKSON	OCTOBER 6, 1896
KNEADING MACHINE	J. LEE	AUGUST 7, 1895
LAWN MOWER	J. A. BURR	MAY 9, 1899
LEMON SQUEEZER	J. T. WHITE	DECEMBER 8, 1886
LIBRARY TABLE	W. DAVIS, JR.	SEPTEMBER 24, 1878
LOCK	W. A. MARTIN	JULY 23, 1889
LUBRICATOR	E. J. MC COY	JUNE 16, 1885
LUGGAGE CARRIER	J. W. BUTTS	OCTOBER 10, 1899

PRODUCT	BLACK INVENTOR	DATE
MOTOR	J. GREGORY	APRIL 26, 1887
NAILING MACHINE	J. E. MATZELIGER	FEB. 25, 1896
OIL CUP	E. J. MC COY	NOVEMBER 15, 1898
OIL STOVE	J. STANDARD	OCTOBER 29, 1889
PENCIL SHARPENER	J. L. LOVE	NOVEMBER 23, 1897
PHOTO EMBOSSING MACHINE	C. J. DORTICUS	APRIL 16, 1895
PHOTO PRINT WASH	C. J. DORTICUS	APRIL 23, 1895
PORTABLE SCALES	J. H. HUNTER	NOVEMBER 3, 1896
PRINTING PRESS	W. A. LAVALETTE	SEPTEMBER 17,, 1878
PROPELLER FOR VESSELS	G. TOLIVER	APRIL 28, 1891
RAILROAD SWITCH	C. V. RICHEY	AUGUST 3, 1897
RAILWAY SIGNAL	A. B. BLACKBURN	JANUARY 10, 1888
REFRIGERATOR	J. STANDARD	JULY 14, 1891
REGISTERS	A. F. HILYER	OUTOBER 14, 1890
RIDING SADDLES	W. D. DAVIS	OCTOBER 6, 1896
ROTARY ENGINE	A. J. BEARD	JULY 5, 1892
SHAMPOO HEADREST	C. O. BAILIFF	OCTOBER 11, 1898
SHOE LASTING MACHINE	J. E. MATZELIGER	SEPTEMBER 22, 1891
SHUTTER & FASTENING	J. COOPER	MAY 1, 1883
SNOW MELTING APPARATUS	F. J. FERRELL	MAY 27, 1890
SPRINKLER FOR LAWNS	J. W. SMITH	MAY 4, 1897
STEAM BOILER FURNACE	G. T.WOODS	JUNE 3, 1884
STOVE	T. A. CARRINGTON	JULY 25, 1876
STRAIGHTENING COMB	MADAM C. J. WALKER	APPROX 1905
STREET CAR FENDER	M. A. CHERRY	JANUARY 1, 1895
STREET LETTER BOX	P. B. DOWNING	OCTOBER 27, 1891
STREET SPRINKLING	M. W. BINGA	JULY 22, 1879

PRODUCT	BLACK INVENTOR	DATE
STREET SWEEPER	CHARLES B. BROOKS	MARCH 17, 1896
SUGAR EVAPORATING PAN	NORBET RILLIEUX	DECEMBER 10, 1846
TELEPHONE TRANSMITTER	GRANVILLE T. WOODS	DECEMBER 2, 1884
THERMOSTAT CONTROL	FREDERICK M. JONES	FEBRUARY 23, 1960
TICKET DISPENSING MAC.	FREDERICK M. JONES	JUNE 27, 1939
TRAFFIC LIGHT	GARRETT MORGAN	NOVEMBER 20, 1923
TRAIN ALARM	R. A. BUTLER	JUNE 15, 1897
UMBRELLA STAND	W. C. CARTER	AUGUST 4, 1885
WAGON	J. W. WEST	OCTOBER 18, 1870

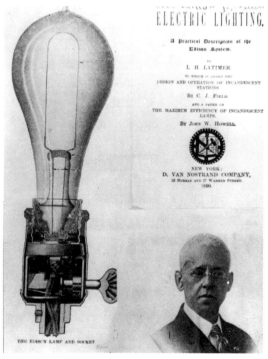

Latimer wrote the 1st book on electric lighting

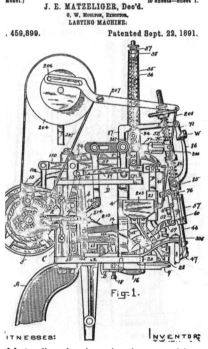

Matzeliger's shoe-lasting machine

REFERENCES AND ADDITIONAL READING

Adams, R. (1969) <u>Great Negroes Past and Present</u>. Chicago: Afro-Am Publishing Co.

Burt, M. (1989) <u>Black Inventors of America.</u> Portland: National Book Co.

Diggs, I. (1975) <u>Black Innovations.</u> Chicago: Institute of Positive Education.

Haber, L. (1970) <u>Black Pioneers of Science and Invention</u>. New York: Harcourt, Brace and World, Inc.

Harris, M. (1964) <u>Black Inventors: The Revolutionary Period</u>. New York: Negro History Associates.

Harris, M. (1964) <u>Early American Inventors, 18th and 19th Centuries.</u> New York: Negro History Associates.

Harris, M. (1974) <u>Granville T. Woods Memorial: Collector's Edition</u>. New York: Negro History Associates.

Hayden, R. (1992) <u>9 African American Inventors</u>. Frederick, Maryland: Twenty-First Century Books.

Klein, A. (1971) <u>The Hidden Contributions: Black Scientists and Inventors in America</u>. New York: Doubleday and Co.

Latimer, L. (1890) <u>Incandescent Electric Lighting: A Practical Description of the Edison System</u>. New York: D. Van Norstrand Co.

Rogers, J. (1989) <u>Africa's Gift to America</u>. St. Petersburg, FL: Helga Rogers Publishing.

Van Sertima, I. (1983) <u>Blacks in Science Ancient and Modern</u>. New Brunswick, NJ: Transaction Books.

WEST POINT ACADEMY AND BLACK CADETS

President Thomas Jefferson, under an 1802 Act of Congress, initially established the U.S. Military at West Point, New York, as a corps of engineers. General Sylvanus Thayer was appointed superintendent in 1814, and became known as the "Father of West Point" because of his academic expansion. Since members of Congress had to nominate West Point cadets, no African Americans were nominated until the Reconstruction period when Black voters elected Black Congressmen. The 13th, 14th, and 15th constitutional amendments made election of Black Congressmen possible. Emancipation was accomplished by the 13th amendment (1865); citizenship through the 14th amendment (1868); and the 15th amendment granted suffrage to Black males (1870).

African American Congressmen nominated 27 Blacks to West Point Academy between 1870 and 1887. Only twelve members of the group passed the academic and physical examinations for admission. Academically, they were examined in mathematics (including fractions and decimals) in addition to the rules of correct grammar. Candidates also had to demonstrate knowledge of "U.S. and world geography, by discussing various historical periods, wars, and U.S. administrations." The physical examination required the absence of infectious and chronic disease. During the four-year program, the cadets studied French, Spanish, chemistry, engineering, philosophy, law, mathematics (including calculus), mineralogy, and geology. Despite the many nominations, only three African Americans graduated from West Point Academy during its first 130 years of existence.

The first African American nominated to West Point was James Webster Smith who attended from 1870, until January 1874. James Smith was described as "a hot headed activist, bent on righting the wrongs of racial inequality." Smith was forced to repeat his first year at West Point because of an alleged lie in response to a charge of inattention in the ranks. After his fourth year, Smith wrote his patron, David Clark of Connecticut, complaining about the academy's mistreatment of Black cadets. His letters sparked a congressional board of inquiry, which eventually recommended the court martial of several White cadets. However, since one of the White cadets was the nephew of William Belknap, Secretary of War, the punishment was reduced to a mere reprimand. Smith's personal and public need to eradicate social injustice at West Point Academy resulted in extreme classmate hatred and the eventual dismissal of Smith from the academy for fighting, after a court martial and three-week imprisonment.

Johnson Chesnut Whittaker was chosen to fill the vacancy created by James Smith's dismissal. Contrary to Smith, Whittaker was described as a quiet, shy, cowardly student who sought solace in the Bible. After completing four years and just prior to his final examinations, Whittaker was found on the floor of his room, "bleeding and insensible, bound hand and foot to his bedstead. His head was partly shaved, and his feet and hands slashed." Whittaker claimed that three masked men were responsible, and this created such uproar in the press that Congress initiated another investigation. A court of inquiry accused Whittaker of self-mutilation to avoid his final examinations. He received a court marital and was sentenced to a dishonorable discharge from the military, and one year hard labor in prison. President Chester Arthur reversed the entire proceedings but did not allow him to finish West Point.

Henry Flipper, a former slave, was a roommate of both James Smith and Johnson Whittaker and was determined to finish West Point Academy at all costs. Henry received his appointment to West Point Academy upon the recommendation of Congressman James Freeman, who needed the Black vote for re-election. Despite threats, bribes as high as $5,000, and refusal of any cadets to speak to him for four years, Flipper became the first Black West Point graduate on June 14, 1877. Prominent Blacks throughout the nation were proud of Flipper's accomplishment

Henry O. Flipper

and Charles Douglass, son of Frederick Douglass, sponsored a New York City reception in his honor.

On January 2, 1878, Flipper received his commission as second lieutenant and was assigned to the all Black 10th U.S. Calvary (called the Buffalo Soldiers) at Fort Sill, Oklahoma. Henry Flipper performed exceptionally well during his first four years and was well liked by everyone. He served admirably in a number of combat assignments on the frontier and also

Buffalo Soldiers

Eighty Black cadets graduated in West Point Academy's Class of 2000

THE LATE
Col.
Charles
Young

RESCUED TEDDY
ROOSEVELT AND
HIS FAMOUS
"ROUGH RIDERS"
AT SAN JUAN
HILL.

WEST POINT GRADUATE
MILITARY ATTACHE
HAITI, LIBERIA.

SPINGARN MEDAL
·1915·

Only three African Americans graduated from West Point Academy during its first 130 years of existence: Henry Flipper (1877), John Alexander (1887), and Charles Young (1894). Alexander died on duty in 1894. Young retired, with honors, as a Colonel.

worked brilliantly as an engineer. He designed and perfected a drainage system that eliminated diseased stagnant rainwater (and subsequently malaria) that was plaguing the fort. Still known as "Flipper's Ditch", it became a national landmark in 1977. Unfortunately, he was transferred to Fort Davis, Texas in 1881 commanded by the racist Colonel William Shafter. Shafter disliked Blacks in general and the Buffalo Soldiers in particular. Shortly after Lieutenant Flipper's arrival, he was accused of stealing commissary funds. Flipper stated at his court martial that he hid the funds in his personal trunk because there was no secure place to keep the commissary funds and that Colonel Shafter was fully aware of this. Despite the fact that Colonel Shafter had Lucy Smith, Flipper's White housekeeper, laundress, and cook searched, and that $2,800 in commissary checks were found in her blouse, this fact was never mentioned at the trial. Moreover, the local town merchants, who highly admired Flipper, took up a collection and replaced all the missing funds. The court martial panel could not convict Flipper of embezzlement but was able to convict him of "conduct unbecoming an officer and gentleman." Although the Army's judge advocate general concluded that the conviction was racially motivated, President Chester Arthur refused to reverse his conviction, and Flipper was dishonorably discharged.

Henry Flipper used his outstanding education at West Point Academy to carve out a distinguished career as a civil and mining engineer, especially in and around Mexico, since he had learned fluent Spanish. He initially worked for an American mining company surveying land in Mexico. When Texas and Arizona joined the United States, Flipper translated Spanish land deeds and titles for the Land Grant Court, and investigated their authenticity in Mexico City records. Flipper later joined the Justice Department and Senate Foreign Relations Committee as an expert on Mexican political developments. Subsequently, Secretary of Interior, Albert Fall, a close friend of Henry Flipper, chose him as chief civil engineer in determining the course for the Alaskan railroad lines.

Flipper unsuccessfully devoted his entire life to clearing his name. Four bills were introduced in Congress between 1903 and 1908 to clear Flipper, but racist Southern politicians allowed the bills to die in committee. Despite all of his accomplishments, he died bitterly disappointed in 1940, at age 84. The redemption of Flipper's name was rekindled by a schoolteacher from Valdosta, Georgia named Ray MacColl, who learned about Flipper while taking a Black history course and embarked on a tireless campaign to right what he regarded as a major injustice. Through MacColl's efforts, the Army's Board for the Correction of Military Records reviewed the circumstances of Flipper's discharge and changed his discharge from dishonorable to honorable in 1976. Moreover, in 1977, exactly 100 years after his graduation, the Henry O. Flipper Memorial Award was established at West Point Academy and is given annually to the cadet who best demonstrates leadership, self discipline, and perseverance. On February 11, 1978, his remains were moved from an unmarked grave in Atlanta and reburied, with full military honors in his hometown of Thomasville, Georgia.

On February 19, 1999, President Clinton granted Henry Flipper the first post-humorous pardon in American history, calling the pardon "an event that is 117 years overdue." Retired General Colin Powell, who attended the pardon ceremony, kept a picture of Flipper on the wall of his office at the Pentagon when he was Chairman of the Joint Chief of Staff. Powell wrote in his autobiography: "We knew that the path through the underbrush of prejudice and discrimination had been cleared by the sacrifices of nameless Blacks who had gone before us, the Henry Flippers...and to them we owed everything."

Henry Flipper is now a revered figure at West Point where a memorial bust is dedicated to him in the cadet library. Eighty Black cadets graduated in West Point Academy's class of 2000, and they should never forget that African Americans "stand tall because we stand on the shoulders of those who came before us." Pioneers are those with "arrows in their backs", and we must never stop honoring our pioneers.

REFERENCES AND ADDITIONAL READING

Ambrose, S. (1966) <u>Duty, Honor, Country: A History of West Point.</u> Baltimore: The Johns Hopkins Press.

Black, L. & Black, S. (1985) <u>An Officer and a Gentleman: The Military Career of Henry O. Flipper</u>. Dayton, Ohio: The Lora Co.

Donaldson, G. (1991) <u>The History of African-Americans in the Military</u>. Malabar, FL: Krieger Publishing Co.

Eppinga, J. (1996) <u>Henry Ossian Flipper</u>. Plano, Texas: Republic of Texas Press.

Flipper, H. (1878) <u>The Colored Cadet at West Point. Autobiography of Lieut. Henry Ossian Flipper</u>. New York: Homer Lee & Co.

Foner, J. (1974) <u>Blacks and the Military in American History.</u> New York: A New Perspective Publishing Co.

Glass, E. (1921) <u>History of the Tenth Cavalry.</u> Tucson: Acme Printing Co.

Greene, R. (1974) <u>Black Defenders of America: 1775-1973.</u> Chicago: Johnson Publishing.

Harris, T. (ed.) (1963) <u>Negro Frontiersman: The Western Memoirs of Henry O. Flipper</u>. El Paso: Texas Western College Press.

Lanning, M. (1997) <u>The African-American Soldier From Crispus Attucks to Colin Powell</u>. Secaucus, NJ: Carol Publishing Group.

Mullen, R. (1973) <u>Blacks in America's Wars.</u> New York: Pathfinder.

Nalty, B. (1986) <u>Strength for the Fight: A History of Black Americans in the Military</u>. New York: Free Press.

BROWNSVILLE, TEXAS AND BLACK SOLDIERS

Despite stellar performances through five previous wars, Black servicemen in the early 1900s were hated by the South and despised and unappreciated by the North. Southerners hated Blacks in uniform because radical Republicans in Congress had used Black soldiers to police the South during Reconstruction and as added humiliation after their Civil War defeat. After Reconstruction, Black soldiers were sent to the Western frontier to fight "hostile Indians," but found the environment of White racism tremendously more hostile than the Native Americans. Nothing more typified American racial hatred for the Black soldier than the "Brownsville Affair".

Black Servicemen were hated in the South after reconstruction.

President Theodore Roosevelt without a formal trial or the benefit of legal counsel discharged all 167 soldiers.

During the summer of 1906, the first battalion of the 25th infantry regiment was transferred from Fort Niobrara in Nebraska, to Fort Brown, a post near Brownsville, Texas (at the mouth of the Rio Grande River) to protect against Mexican revolutionaries. These 167 men had outstanding credentials for service, loyalty, discipline, and bravery during battles fought in Cuba and the Philippines. Six of these Black soldiers held the Medal of Honor and 13 had been awarded citations for bravery in the Spanish-American War. More than half of the soldiers had been in uniform for more than five years; 25 had served in active duty for more than ten years; and one had accrued more that 27 years. The citizens of Brownsville were appalled and wrote William Howard Taft, the Secretary of War, requesting that he keep the White 26th infantry at Fort Brown instead. The War Department refused to repeal the order and responded to the Brownsville citizens: "The fact is that a certain amount of race prejudice between Whites and Blacks seems to have become almost universal throughout the country, and no matter where Colored troops are sent there are always some who make objections to their coming."

The Brownsville citizens immediately posted new signs announcing **"NO NIGGERS OR DOGS ALLOWED"** on saloons, restaurants, and all public and recreational facilities.   However, since Brownsville is located near the Mexican border, most of the town's inhabitants were low paid Mexican workers, and these Hispanics welcomed the soldiers at their establishments.   Consequently, Whites became very concerned that the assertive Black infantrymen might inspire Mexicans to challenge the status quo of White dominance and to resist local Jim Crow practices. As much as the White citizens of Brownsville hated Black soldiers, they saw an interracial alliance as an even greater threat to their town and felt compelled to eliminate the Black military presence by whatever means necessary.

Shortly after midnight on August 14, 1906, a group of men across the road from Fort Brown, and dressed in army uniforms, began firing shots randomly into buildings and at streetlights for about ten minutes. The random bullets killed a bartender, and seriously wounded a police lieutenant. Military rifle cartridges and clips from Springfield rifles recently issued to the 25th regiment were found at the scene.   Several Brownsville citizens immediately claimed that they saw Blacks shooting. Major Penrose said it could not have been Black soldiers because all the battalion's soldiers were accounted for by company commanders at the 10:00 PM curfew check and again immediately after the shooting. The rifles were also checked and none had been recently fired.   The Major stated that anyone could wear an army uniform because old uniforms were routinely discarded outside the fort, and that ammunition and rifles were known to have been sold to the citizens of Brownsville by the White 26th regiment that occupied the fort before the Black soldiers.   Brownsville Mayor, Fred Come, organized an investigating committee of local citizens who found witnesses who professed to have heard voices that sounded Black. Five witnesses said they saw Black soldiers but could not identify anyone, and they were not under oath. The committee prefaced their questions by stating: "We know that this outrage was committed by Negro soldiers. We want any information that will lead to a discovery of who did it." The committee did not call a single soldier to the inquiry.

After one day of testimony, the committee sent a telegram to President Theodore Roosevelt stating: "Our women and children are terrified and our men practically under constant alarm and watchfulness. No community can stand this strain...we ask you to have the troops at once removed from Fort Brown and replaced by White soldiers." President Roosevelt ordered two investigations, one by Major August Blocksom and a second by General Ernest Garlington, a racist native of South Carolina. They took as evidence the testimony of White citizens and spent military cartridges and concurred that Black soldiers had committed the crime. They completely ignored the testimony of a civilian employee of the fort who swore that after the shooting he had seen four Brownsville citizens dressed in uniforms and carrying rifles. The officers concluded that the Black soldiers' denial of the shooting was proof of "collusion" and a "conspiracy-of-silence" and since no soldier would confess, they recommended dismissing the entire battalion. General Garlington added: "The secretive nature of the race, where crimes charged to members of their color are made, is well known."

Theodore Roosevelt delayed his decision until after his re-election so as not to lose much needed Black support. Subsequently, on November 28, 1906, he ordered the discharge of all 167 soldiers of the first battalion without honor, and he denied the soldiers all back pay and pension benefits. The soldiers never received a formal trial or the benefit of legal counsel, and this remains the only example of mass punishment without the benefit of trial in U.S. military history. White people across the country celebrated Roosevelt's decision. The "New Orleans Picayune" reported: "Whatever may be the value of the Negro troops in time of war, the fact remains they are a curse to the country in time of peace." In December 1906, during the first congressional session after the Brownsville incident, Congressman John Garner of Texas, whose district included Brownsville, introduced a bill that "called for elimination of all Blacks currently in the military and barring Black enlistment." Although his bill was defeated, he re-introduced similar bills in each of the next three sessions. Franklin Roosevelt rewarded Garner's racial hatred by selecting him as his vice president in 1932 and 1936.

Senator Joseph Foraker of Ohio tried to rally support without success for the Black soldiers and even proposed a bill providing the men an opportunity to re-enlist. Foraker's defense of the Brownsville soldiers and criticism of the White House "so infuriated" Theodore Roosevelt that the President proceeded to "hound the Senator from public life." However, 66 years later (March 1971), Black California Congressman Augustus Hawkins introduced legislation to amend the records of the 25th regiment to "honorable discharge". On December 6, 1972, President Nixon signed a bill authorizing a one-time pension payment of $25,000 to 86 year old Dorsie Willis, the only survivor among those discharged, and thus, partially corrected one of the greatest injustices in military history.

REFERENCES AND ADDITIONAL READING

Donaldson, G. (1991) The History of African-Americans in the Military. Malabar, FL: Krieger Publishing Co.

Foner, J. (1974) Blacks and the Military in American History. New York: A New Perspective Publishing Co.

Greene, R. (1974) Black Defenders of America: 1775-1973. Chicago: Johnson Publishing.

Lane, A. (1971) The Brownsville Affair: National Crisis and Black Reaction. Port Washington, NY: National University Publications.

Lanning, M. (1997) The African-American Soldier From Crispus Attucks to Colin Powell. Secaucus, NJ: Carol Publishing Group.

Moebs, T. (1994) Black Soldiers-Black Sailors-Black Ink: Research Guide on African - Americans in U.S. Military History. Chesapeake Bay, MD: Moebs Publishing Co.

Mullen, R. (1973) Blacks in America's Wars. New York: Pathfinder.

Nalty, B. (1986) Strength for the Fight: A History of Black Americans in the Military. New York: Free Press.

Weaver, J. (1970) The Brownsville Raid. New York: W.W. Norton.

AFTER 1900

BLACK SCIENTISTS

In a review of historical literature, one is appalled by the absence of serious attention given to Black scientists by American historians. Yet, the collective contribution of Black Americans to science is so extensive that it is not possible to live a full day in any part of the United States, or the world for that matter, without sharing in the benefits of their contributions in such fields as: biology, chemistry, physics, space, and nuclear science.

The first scientific book ever written by an African American is believed to be the astronomical <u>Almanac</u> published by Benjamin Banneker in 1792; and he continued to publish an almanac for the next ten years. Banneker's <u>Almanac</u> sold very well among White farmers and was extremely accurate in predicting: eclipses, high and low tides, positions of planets, times for sunrise and sunset, and many other useful items of information. Thomas Jefferson was so impressed by this self-taught mathematical genius that he sent a copy of Banneker's <u>Almanac</u> to the Academy of Sciences in Paris to prove that the color of a person's skin had nothing to do with intelligence. Jefferson also had Benjamin Banneker appointed to the Federal Commission which planned and laid out Washington, D.C. When the head of the commission, Pierre L'Enfant, angrily quit and took all the plans back to France, Banneker was the only one able to reproduce the entire map and layout from memory; thus allowing our nation's capital to be completed.

The first national monument ever erected in honor of an African American was erected for George Washington Carver. A postage stamp was also issued in his honor. George Washington Carver, a former slave, was among the most outstanding agricultural scientists in the world. When the boll weevil completely destroyed the Southern cotton industry, Carver saved the Southern economy from financial ruin by convincing the farmers to grow peanuts instead. Moreover, his scientific research was able to create more than 300 products from the peanut and its shell.

George Washington Carver

USS George Washington Carver: A nuclear-powered
Ballistic-Missile submarine commissioned in June 1966

George Washington Carver was also an expert in detecting and treating plant diseases and was a collaborator for the U.S. Bureau of Plant Industry. Thomas Edison and Henry Ford both offered Carver large sums of money to work for them, but he never left his teaching position at Tuskegee Institute.

Percy Lavon Julian

Percy Lavon Julian was one of America's premier chemists. His scientific work ranged from developing new substances that snuffed out gasoline and oil fires to synthesizing the drug Cortisone, which eases the pain of people with Rheumatoid Arthritis. Julian received 105 U.S. patents for chemical products and processes including two patents for his synthesis of male and female sex hormones called testosterone and progesterone. After working 17 years as Director of Research at the Glidden Chemical Company of Chicago, Illinois, he founded the Julian Laboratories Incorporated in 1954, with plants in Chicago, Illinois and Guatemala, Mexico. His plants became immensely successful and in 1961, Julian sold the Guatemala plant to

Charles Drew surgeon known also for his success with the Blood Bank

the Upjohn Company, and the Chicago plant to Smith, Kline and French Company. Percy Julian succeeded as a major contributor to science despite the extreme hardships he endured because of his race, including the fact that he had to obtain his Ph.D. from the University of Vienna in Austria because American universities would not accept him.

Another famous African American scientist is Charles R. Drew who made possible the availability of stored blood plasma for blood transfusions. He was the first to preserve blood plasma for long periods of time with his researched method of careful storage and refrigeration. Before Dr. Drew's research, blood could not be stored for longer than 24 hours. Moreover, Dr. Drew's research allowed thousands of units of blood to be donated and preserved for use by our military during World War II.

Dr. William Hinton devoted 30 years to research on syphilis. In 1935, the "Hinton Test" for syphilis was adopted by the entire state of Massachusetts, and in 1936 Hinton's book <u>Syphilis and its Treatment</u> became the first medical textbook written by an African American, ever published.

Famous Black physicists include Dr. Lloyd Quarterman who helped develop the atomic bomb and the first nuclear reactor for atomic powered submarines. Christine Darden was the leading NASA researcher in supersonic aircraft with expertise in the area of reducing sonic boom.

Despite the fact that only about three percent of American scientists have been Black, they have made tremendous contributions for the benefit and betterment of mankind. It is truly a crime that the genius and imagination of the African American scientist is generally unknown to most Americans, both Black and White.

Willie "C" Jackson
1531 W. 64th Street
Los Angeles CA. 90047

REFERENCES AND ADDITIONAL READING

Adams, R. (1969) <u>Great Negroes Past and Present</u>. Chicago: Afro-Am Publishing Co.

Bedini, S. (1972) <u>The Life of Benjamin Banneker</u>. New York: Charles Scribner's Sons.

Diggs, I. (1975) <u>Black Innovations.</u> Chicago: Institute of Positive Education.

Haber, L. (1970) <u>Black Pioneers of Science and Invention</u>. New York: Harcourt, Brace and World Inc.

Hayden, R. (1992) <u>11 African American Doctors.</u> Frederick, Maryland: Twenty-First Century Books.

Hayden, R. (1992) <u>7 African American Scientists</u>. Frederick, Maryland: Twenty-First Century Books.

Holt, R. (1943) <u>George Washington Carver: An American Biography.</u> New York: Doubleday & Co.

Jay, J. (1971) <u>Negroes in Science: Natural Science Doctorates 1876-1969</u>. Detroit: Balamp Publishing Co.

Klein, A. (1971) <u>The Hidden Contributions: Black Scientists and Inventors in America.</u> New York: Doubleday & Co.

Lewis, C. (1970) <u>Benjamin Banneker: The Man Who Saved Washington</u>. New York: McGraw-Hill.

Van Sertima, I. (1983) <u>Blacks in Science Ancient and Modern.</u> New Brunswick, NJ: Transaction Books.

Winslow, E. (ed.) (1974) <u>Black Americans in Science and in Engineering: Contributions of Past and Present</u>. Chicago: Afro-Am Publishing Co.

THE BLACK (NEGRO) WALL STREET

The "Black (Negro) Wall Street" was the name given to Greenwood Avenue of North Tulsa, Oklahoma during the early 1900's. Because of strict segregation, Blacks were only allowed to shop, spend, and live in a 35 square block area called the Greenwood District. The "circulation of Black dollars" only in the Black community produced a tremendously prosperous Black business district that was admired and envied by the whole country.

Oklahoma's first African-American settlers were Indian slaves of the so-called "Five Civilized Tribes": Chickasaws, Choctaws, Cherokees, Creeks, and Seminoles. These tribes were forced to leave the Southeastern United States and resettle in Oklahoma, in mid-winter, over the infamous "Trail of Tears." After the Civil War, U.S.-Indian treaties provided for slave liberation and land allotments ranging from 40-100 acres, which helps explain why over 6,000 African-Americans lived in the Oklahoma territory by 1870. Oklahoma boasted of more all-Black towns and communities than any other state in the land, and these communities opened their arms to freed slaves from all across the country. Remarkably, at one time, there were over 30 African-American newspapers in Oklahoma.

Tulsa began as an outpost of the Creek Indians and, as late as 1910, Walter White of the NAACP, described Tulsa as "the dead and hopeless home of 18,182 souls." Suddenly, oil was discovered and Tulsa rapidly grew into a thriving, bustling, enormously wealthy town of 73,000 by 1920, with bank deposits totaling over $65 million. However, Tulsa was a "tale of two cities isolated and insular", one Black and one White. Tulsa was so racist and segregated that it was the only city in America that boasted of segregated telephone booths.

Since African Americans could neither live among Whites as equals, nor patronize White businesses in Tulsa, Blacks had to develop a completely separate business district and community, which soon became prosperous and legendary. Black dollars invested in the Black community also produced self-pride, self-sufficiency, and self-determination. The business district, beginning at the intersection of Greenwood Avenue and Archer Street, became so successful and vibrant that Booker T. Washington during his visit bestowed the moniker: "Negro Wall Street." By 1921, Tulsa's African-American population of 11,000 had its own bus line, two high schools, one hospital, two newspapers, two theaters, three drug stores, four hotels, a public library, and thirteen churches. In addition, there were over 150 two and three story brick commercial buildings that housed clothing and grocery stores, cafes, rooming houses, nightclubs, and a large number of professional offices including doctors, lawyers, and dentists. Tulsa's progressive African American community boasted some of the city's most elegant brick homes, well furnished with china, fine linens, beautiful furniture, and grand pianos. Mary Elizabeth Parrish from Rochester, New York wrote: "In the residential section there were homes of beauty and splendor which would please the most critical eye." Well known African American personalities often visited the Greenwood district including: educators Mary McCloud Bethune and W.E.B. DuBois, scientist George Washington Carver, opera singer Marian Anderson, blues singer Dinah Washington, and noted Chicago chemist Percy Julian.

T.P. Scott wrote in "Negro City Directory": "Early African American business leaders in Tulsa patterned the development of Tulsa's thriving Greenwood district after the successful African American entrepreneurial activity in Durham, North Carolina." After the Civil War, former slaves moved to Durham from the neighboring farmlands and found employment in tobacco processing plants. By 1900, a large Black middle class had developed which began businesses that soon grew into phenomenally successful corporations, especially North Carolina Mutual Life Insurance Company. Charles Clinton Spaulding was so successful with the North Carolina Mutual Life Insurance Company that he was able to create a real estate company, a textile and hosiery mill, and the "Durham Negro Observer" newspaper.

Durham Blacks also created a hospital, Mechanics and Farmers Bank (1908), North Carolina Training College (1910), Banker's Fire Insurance Company (1920), and the National Negro Finance Company (1922). However, living conditions in Durham were so sub-standard, and working conditions so poor that the 1920 mortality rate among Blacks in Durham was three times higher than that of Whites. As of 1926, 64% of all African Americans in Durham died before the age of 40. These perilous working and living conditions were not present in Tulsa.

Tulsa riots

On May 31, 1921, the successful Black Greenwood district was completely destroyed by one of the worse race riots in U.S. history. A 19 year old Black male accidentally stumbled on a jerky elevator and bumped the 17-year-old White elevator operator, who screamed. The frightened young fellow was seen running

"Charred Negro" The burned body of a Black man killed during the Tulsa Race Riot

from the elevator by a group of Whites and, by late afternoon the "Tulsa Tribune" reported that the girl had been raped. Despite the girl's denial of any wrongdoing, the boy was arrested and a large mob of 2,000 White men came to the jail to lynch the prisoner. About 75 armed African Americans came to the jail to offer assistance to the sheriff to protect the prisoner. The sheriff not only refused the assistance but also deputized the White mob to disarm the Blacks. With a defenseless Black community before them, the White mob advanced to the Greenwood district where they first looted and then burned all Black businesses, homes, and churches.

Any Black resisters were shot and thrown into the fires. When the National Guard arrived, they assisted the others by arresting all Black men, women, and children, and herding them into detention centers at the Baseball Park and Convention Hall. As many as 4,000 Blacks were held under armed guard in detention. Dr. Arthur C. Jackson, a nationally renowned surgeon, and called by the Mayo brothers (of Mayo Clinic fame) "the most able Negro surgeon in America", was shot at the Convention Hall and allowed to bleed to death. The Chicago Tribune Newspaper reported that Whites also used private airplanes to drop kerosene and dynamite on Black homes. By the next morning the entire Greenwood district was reduced to ashes and not one White was even accused of wrongdoing, much less arrested.

Tulsa riots

The race riot of Tulsa, Oklahoma was not an isolated event in American history. On May 28, 1917, a White mob of over 3,000, in East St. Louis, Illinois ravaged African American stores, homes, and churches. Eyewitnesses reported that over 100 Blacks were gunned down as they left their burning homes, including a small Black child who was shot and thrown back into the burning building to die. Seven White police officers, charged with murder by the Illinois Attorney General, were collectively fined $150. During the "Red Summer" of 1919, over 25 race riots, where White mobs attacked Black neighborhoods, were recorded. In the 1919 race riot at Elaine, Arkansas, White mobs killed over 200 African Americans and burned their

Practicing law from a tent

homes and businesses. Federal troops arrested hundreds of Blacks trying to protect their possessions and forcibly held them in basements of the city's public schools. Twelve Blacks were indicted (no Whites) and convicted of inciting violence and sentenced to die. The NAACP persuaded the U.S. Supreme Count, for the first time in history, to reverse a racially biased Southern court.

Director John Singleton exposed the horror of the Rosewood, Florida massacre of 1922, in his film entitled "Rosewood". A White mob burned down the entire town and tried to kill all of its Black inhabitants. In April 1994, the Florida legislature passed the "Rosewood Bill", which awarded $150,000 to each of the riot's nine eligible Black survivors.

After the Tulsa riot, the White inhabitants tried to buy the Black property and force Black people out of town. No Tulsa bank or lending institution would make loans in the riot-marred Greenwood district, and the city refused all outside assistance. However, racial pride and self-determination would not permit the Greenwood owners to sell, and they doggedly spent the entire winter in tents donated by the American Red Cross.

Rebuilding was a testament to the courage and stamina of Tulsa's pioneers in their struggle for freedom. Most of the buildings along the first block of Greenwood Avenue were rebuilt within one year. Henry Whitlow wrote: "A little over a decade after the riot, everything was more prosperous than before."

Black Wall Street Memorial

In 1926, W.E.B. DuBois visited Tulsa and wrote: "Black Tulsa is a happy city. It has new clothes. It is young and gay and strong. Five little years ago, fire and blood and robbery leveled it to the ground. Scars are there, but the city is impudent and noisy. It believes in itself. Thank God for the grit of Black Tulsa." Like Black Tulsa, African Americans can continue to survive by self-pride, self-help, and self-determination.

Black Wall Street Re-built

REFERENCES AND ADDITIONAL READING

Brown, R. (1975) <u>Strain of Violence: Historical Studies of American Violence and Virgilantism</u>. New York: Oxford University Press.

Butler, W. (1974) <u>Tulsa 75: A History of Tulsa.</u> Tulsa: Metropolitan Tulsa Chamber of Commerce.

Debo, A. (1982) <u>Tulsa: From Creek Town to Oil Capital</u>. Norman: University of Oklahoma Press.

Ellsworth, S. (1943) <u>Death in a Promised Land: The Tulsa Race Riot of 1921</u>. Baton Rouge: Louisiana State University Press.

Franklin, J. (1974) <u>From Slavery to Freedom: A History of Negro Americans</u>. New York: Alfred Knopf.

Franklin, J. (1980) <u>The Blacks in Oklahoma</u>. Norman: University of Oklahoma Press.

Gates, E. (1997) <u>They Came Searching-How Blacks Sought the Promised Land in Tulsa.</u> Austin, Texas: Eakin Press.

Johnson, H. (1998) <u>Black Wall Street: From Riot to Renaissance in Tulsa's Historic Greenwood District</u>. Austin, Texas: Eakin Press.

Teall, K. (1971) <u>Black History in Oklahoma: A Resource Book</u>. Oklahoma City: Oklahoma City Public Schools.

Waskow, A. (1967) <u>From Race Riot to Sit-In, 1919 and the 1960's: A Study in the Connections Between Conflict and Violence</u>. Garden City, NY: Doubleday.

Williams, L. (1972) <u>Anatomy of Four Race Riots-Racial Conflict in Knoxville, Elaine (Arkansas), Tulsa, and Chicago</u>. The University and College Press of Mississippi.

MARCUS MOSIAH GARVEY

Marcus Garvey

Marcus Mosiah Garvey (1887-1940) arrived in the United States from Jamaica almost penniless in 1916, but within six years he boasted of an organization with branches worldwide that had over six million registered members. He was almost worshiped by the Black masses throughout the world for his vision to organize the Black race through race pride, education, self-reliance, economic development, and the desire to build a strong African motherland controlled by Africans. Garvey wrote: "I read Booker T. Washington's <u>Up From Slavery</u> and then my doom–if I may so call it–of being a race leader dawned upon me. I asked, Where is the Black man's government? Where is his king and kingdom? Where are his president, his country, his ambassadors, his army, his navy, and his men of big affairs? I could not find them. I decided, I will help to make them."

Marcus Garvey founded the Universal Negro Improvement Association (UNIA) in Harlem, in 1918. By 1924, there were over 700 branches in 38 states and over 200 branches throughout the world, as far away as South Africa at a time when there was no E-mail, television, or even radio to advertise. Those who could not hear Garvey directly received his views through his newspaper called the "Negro World", which boasted a circulation as high as 200,000, by 1924. The most recent speeches of Marcus Garvey were published, in addition to articles on race pride, self-reliance, and anti-colonialism. In 1919, the UNIA and "Negro World" were blamed for the numerous violent colonial uprisings in Jamaica, Grenada, Belize, Trinidad, and Tobago. British and French authorities deported all UNIA organizers and banned the "Negro World" from all their colonies, but seamen continued to smuggle the paper throughout the world. In 1921, the U.S. Marines invaded a UNIA meeting in the Dominican Republic and arrested every man, woman, and child in attendance. In Rhodesia (Zimbabwe), in 1927, an African was given life imprisonment for smuggling in only three copies of the newspaper. Although the "Negro World" was banned in Kenya, Jomo Kenyatta, the first president of independent Kenya, told how "someone who could understand English would read Garvey's 'Negro World' message to a group of Africans until they were able to memorize it. They would then spread the message far and wide throughout the countryside."

Garvey Militia

Marcus Garvey in Uniform

Kwame Nkrumah

Jomo Kenyatta

"Race first" was the first major theme of Garvey in his attempt to restore race pride and to destroy the inferiority complex of Black people. Garvey demanded that Black people have Black heroes: "Take down the pictures of White men and women from your walls and elevate your own men and women to that place of honor. Mothers! Give your children dolls that look like them to play with and cuddle." He demanded that his followers abandon skin lighteners and hair straighteners. Garvey said: "God made no mistake when he made us Black with kinky hair...take the kinks out of your minds instead of your hair." In religion, Garvey insisted that Black people should worship images of God and angels that look like them. Marcus Garvey also thought history was extremely important and told his audiences: "We have a beautiful history, and we shall create another one in the future. When savages, heathens, and pagans inhabited Europe, Africa was peopled with a race of cultured Black men, who were masters in art, science, and literature. Whatsoever a Black man has done, a Black man can do."

"Self-reliance and economic development" was Garvey's second major theme. He founded the "Negro Factories Corporation" in 1919, with the ultimate objective of "manufacturing every marketable commodity" and establishing factories throughout the world, which could also employ and train thousands of Black workers. Garvey was proud that his corporate stock was only available to Black people. Yet, he still raised enough money in New York City alone to operate three grocery stores, two restaurants, a printing plant, a steam laundry, and a men and women's manufacturing department that made uniforms, hats, and shirts for such groups as his Black Cross Nurses. Similar enterprises occurred throughout the United States, Central America, and the West Indies. In order to distribute these products worldwide, Marcus Garvey's organization raised enough money within one year (1919) in $5 stock certificates to purchase three ships, which he called the "Black Star Line." Hugh Mulzac, a Black ship's officer, said that hundreds of thousands of people throughout the Western Hemisphere welcomed them as conquering heroes wherever they docked. He wrote: "Thousands of peasants came down from the hills on horses, donkeys, and in makeshift carts, showering us with flowers, fruits, and gifts...we had the first ship they had ever seen entirely owned and operated by Colored men."

"Africa for Africans at home and abroad" was another very strong message from Marcus Garvey. He believed that if Black people could not develop a strong country in Africa, as a protective base, then White people would eventually destroy all Blacks, especially African Americans; just as they had done to the Tasmanians, native Australians, and native Americans. Garvey partitioned the League of Nations, after World War I, to give the African colonies of Germany back to native Africans and to allow the UNIA to serve as custodian. He also negotiated with Liberia for land that could serve as a beachhead for trained African Americans to spread modern technology and scientific skills throughout Africa. Garvey sent thousands of dollars of equipment to Liberia in preparation of transferring his headquarters to Monrovia, but was blocked at the last minute by extreme pressure from the neighboring British and French colonies. Garvey never gave up his dream of an independent African continent and even created the red, black, and green flag, in addition to a national anthem for his future African Republic.

The UNIA held a total of eight international conventions, but none was more spectacular than the first, that was held from August 1-31, 1920. Over 25,000 Black delegates from around the world packed Madison Square Garden, and the surrounding New York streets. Delegates reported to the convention on the problems of their native country and many of their grievances were contained in the "Declaration of Rights of the Negro People of the World." The major demands included: "All persons of African descent anywhere in the world should be accepted as free citizens of Africa; Africans must set out to win justice by whatsoever means possible; Blacks must not be tried by all-White judges and juries; Use of the word 'nigger' must cease; Black history must be taught to Black children; and there must be no taxation without representation."

Black intellectuals, especially W.E.B. DuBois, joined the NAACP and other Garvey haters and demanded that the U.S. Attorney General have Garvey arrested and deported back to Jamaica.   They were exceptionally jealous of Garvey's ability to amass millions of Black supporters and raise millions of dollars while refusing to accept any money from Whites. In 1922, Garvey was arrested and charged with mail fraud while promoting stock for the Black Star Line.   The trial was a complete mockery of justice. Even the judge, Julian Mack, was a member of the NAACP, which instigated Garvey's deportation.   Garvey was given the maximum five-year prison sentence, but worldwide protests forced President Calvin Coolidge to commute his sentence after two years and have him deported. Marcus Garvey moved from Jamaica to London in 1935, and died of a stroke on June 10, 1940.

Upon his death, the man who had led the largest, most widespread, most powerful, and most influential movement among people of African descent in world history was completely ignored in textbooks. Fortunately, his spirit lives through the millions of people he has uplifted. For example, Elijah Muhammad was a former UNIA member and while creating the "Nation of Islam", he adopted many of Garvey's ideas like race first, self-reliance, and a separate Black nation. Ho Chi Minh of Vietnam in his youth was a seaman and once spent several months in New York regularly attending UNIA meetings. Kwame Nkrumah, the first President of Ghana, attended many UNIA meetings as a student in New York, and so admired Garvey that he named Ghana's shipping company the "Black Star Line" after Garvey's line. Tony Martin says: "No power could prevent the influence which Marcus Garvey has continued to exert on organizations and individuals since his death.   As he himself was so fond of saying, 'Truth crushed to earth shall rise again' and 'Up you mighty race you can accomplish what you will.'"

REFERENCES AND ADDITIONAL READING

Adams, R. (1969) Great Negroes Past and Present. Chicago: Afro-Am Publishing Co.

Bennett, L. (1988) Before the Mayflower: A History of Black America. New York: Penguin Books.

Clarke, J. (1974) Marcus Garvey and the Vision of Africa. New York: Random House.

Franklin, J. & Meier, A. (eds.) (1982) Black Leaders of the Twentieth Century. Chicago: University of Illinois Press.

Garvey, A. (1970) Garvey and Garveyism. New York: Collier Books.

Garvey, A. (ed.) (1967) Philosophy and Opinions of Marcus Garvey or Africa for the Africans. London: Frank Cass.

Lewis, R. (1988) Marcus Garvey: Anti-Colonial Champion. Trenton, NJ: Africa World Press Inc.

Martin, T. (1983) Marcus Garvey, Hero: A First Biography. Dover, Massachusetts: The Majority Press.

Martin, T. (1976) Race First: The Ideological and Organizational Struggles of Marcus Garvey and the Universal Negro Improvement Association. Westport, Conn.: Greenwood Press.

Nembhard, L. (1978) Trials and Triumphs of Marcus Garvey. Millwood, NY: Kraus Reprint Co.

Rogers, J. (1972) World's Great Men of Color. New York: Macmillan Publishing Co.

Salley, C. (1993) The Black 100: A Ranking of the Most Influential African-Americans, Past and Present. New York: Carol Publishing Group.

ARTHUR ALFONSO SCHOMBURG: FOREMOST BLACK BIBLIOPHILE

When Arthur Schomburg was a child, his peers frequently teased him about having no history. White classmates told him that Black people had never accomplished anything of note and never would. The young Schomburg asked his teacher where he might find books on Black history and was told there is no such thing. As an extended rebuttal to this teacher, he dedicated his entire life to collecting everything he possibly could that was written by people of African descent. Today, the "Schomburg Center for Research in Black Culture," located at 135th Street and Lenox Avenue in

Authur Alfonso Schomburg

Harlem (New York City), has over 150,000 volumes of Black history and nearly five million artifacts, photographs, magazines, and manuscripts from throughout the world; and has become the Mecca for anyone needing to document or research Black history.

Arthur Alfonso Schomburg (1874-1938) has been called the "Sherlock Holmes of Negro History" because of his uncanny ability to locate extremely rare or "presumed lost" material written by people of African decent. Russell L. Adams states that "at the Schomburg Center, a reader may see copies of the 1792-93 almanacs of Benjamin Banneker; <u>Clotel</u>, the first novel published by an African American; early editions of the poems of Phyllis Wheatley; the addresses and broad sides of free men of color in their conventions of protest; and many other extremely rare Black publications, such as sermons on slavery by ex-slaves." John W. Cromwell, while president of the American Negro Academy, wrote Schomburg on June 17, 1928 highly praising and complimenting him: "You possess some magnetic influence drawing you to these treasures that elude the eager quest of others. How can I adequately express to you my indebtedness for your rescue of Banneker from the seclusion in which he has been for 120 years and the many other valuable manuscripts you have located."

Unlike most of his American bibliophile colleagues, Schomburg wanted to collect material from all great men of color worldwide. At his own expense, he often took extended vacations to Europe, Africa, and South America, in search of books, pamphlets, manuscripts, and etchings. In Seville, Spain, he dug into the original records of the West Indies, which were loosely collected there since Western slavery had originated on the Iberian Peninsula. While in Spain, he also definitely established the fact that two of Spain's noted painters, Juan Pareja and Sebastian Gomez, were men of color. Similarly important discoveries were made in France, Germany, and England. In Africa, he found such things as Zulu nursery rhymes printed in the Bantu language, and books on anthropology, folklore, sociology, and customs of the Congo, Guinea, and Ashanti.

In 1925, Schomburg wrote an essay which was published in "The New Negro," by Alain Locke, explaining why he made such tremendous personal sacrifices in time and money: "History must restore what slavery took away...History must become less a matter of argument and more a matter of record. There is the definite desire and determination to have a history: well documented, widely known (at least within race circles), and administered as a stimulating and inspiring tradition for the coming generations."

The "coming generations" to significantly benefit from Schomburg's repository of information include such leaders as Kwame Nkrumah of Ghana, Nnamdi Azikiwe of

Nigeria, and Tom Mboya of Kenya which indicates the importance of Schomburg's collection in the African decolonization process that began in the 1950s. In the United States the collection was a prominent anchor for the Black intellectual and cultural ferment of the 1960s. John Henrik Clarke, one of our foremost historians, says he provided Malcolm X with research material from the Schomburg collection in his numerous televised debates with Ivy League professors. Dr. Clarke also says he met Schomburg at the age of 18 and credits him with providing the written material that enabled his self-education. More recently, Kareem Abdul Jabbar says it took months of research at the Schomburg Center to permit him to complete his recently published book entitled: Black Profiles in Courage.

Arthur Alfonso Schomburg was born on January 24, 1874 in San Juan, Puerto Rico, to a Black mother and White father, who abandoned the household. Schomburg was primarily self-taught but attended public school in Puerto Rico, and attended St. Thomas College in the Virgin Islands. He arrived in New York, in April 1891, as a Black militant fighting for the independence of Cuba and Puerto Rico, but never stopped collecting books and other materials on African history. In 1911, Schomburg and John Bruce founded the influential "Negro Society for Historical Research" and in 1922, he was elected president of the "American Negro Academy", the first major organization of the Black intelligentsia. J.A. Rogers says, "Schomburg was a walking encyclopedia. Ask him almost any fact about the Negro, and he would be almost sure to know something about it offhand." In 1926, he received the "Harmon Award" for his work on Negro education.

Schomburg also wrote extensively for magazines and newspapers. His most popular articles include "The Collected Poems of Phyllis Wheatley"; "The Life of Placido"; "Racial–Identity -Help to the Study of Negro History"; "Spanish Painters of the School of Seville"; and "Notes on Panama". He was also one of the writers included in an anthology of Negro literature by V.F. Calverton, in 1929.

By 1926, Schomburg had collected over 5,000 items including books, documents, and manuscripts, which were purchased for $10,000 by the Carnegie Corporation and donated to the public library in Harlem that was renamed the "Department of Negro Literature and History." In 1932, the Carnegie Corporation provided a grant to the New York Public Library to hire Schomburg as curator of the materials he had collected. He remained curator until his death on June 10, 1938.

The collection of Arthur Schomburg is now housed in the "Schomburg Center for Research in Black Culture" –which serves as a monument to his influence on the Black experience in America and throughout the world. Schomburg's obsession with making Black history "less a matter of argument and more a matter of record" and to "restore what slavery took away" makes this self-taught lonely visionary of indomitable spirit one whom the world of Black scholarship will forever be immensely indebted.

REFERENCES AND ADDITIONAL READING

Adams, R. (1969) <u>Great Negroes Past and Present</u>. Chicago: Afro-Am Publishing Co.

Bontemps, A. (1972) <u>Harlem Renaissance Remembered</u>. New York: Dodd Mead.

Cannon, C. (1941) <u>American Book Collectors and Collecting from Colonial Times to the Present</u>. New York: H.W. Wilson Co.

Clarke, J. (ed.) <u>Harlem: A Community in Transition.</u> New York: Citadel Press.

Colon, J. (1961) <u>A Puerto Rican in New York</u>. New York: Mainstream Publishers.

Gubert, B. (1982) <u>Early Black Bibliographies, 1863-1918</u>. New York: R.R. Garland Publishing.

Huggins, N. (1971) <u>Harlem Renaissance</u>. New York: Oxford University Press.

Josey, E. (ed.) (1970) <u>The Black Librarian in America</u>. Metuchen, NJ: Scarecrow Press.

Rogers, J. (1972) <u>World's Great Men of Color</u>. New York: Macmillan Publishing Co.

Salley, C. (1993) <u>The Black 100: A Ranking of the Most Influential African-Americans Past and Present</u>. New York: Carol Publishing Group.

Sanchez, K. (1983) <u>From Colonial to Community: The History of the Puerto Rican in New York City, 1917-1948</u>. Westport, Conn.: Greenwood Press.

Sinnette, E. (1989) <u>Arthur Alfonso Schomburg: Black Bibliophile and Collector.</u> Detroit: Wayne State University Press.

Smith, J. (1977) <u>Black Academic Libraries and Research Collections: An Historical Survey</u>. Westport, Conn.: Greenwood Press.

Thorpe, E. (1971) <u>Black Historians: A Critique</u>. New York: William Morow.

DR. CARTER GOODWIN WOODSON

Carter Goodwin Woodson (1875-1950) wrote: "If a race has no history, if it has no worthwhile tradition, it becomes a negligible factor in the thought of the world, and it stands in danger of being exterminated." Woodson saw the educational system of his generation as solely dedicated to the glorification of Europeans and their achievements. Consequently, he dedicated his entire life to informing the masses, both Black and White, about the magnificent history and "worthwhile traditions" of people of African descent.

Carter G. Woodson

Dr. Carter G. Woodson has been called the "Father of Negro History" because of his pioneering efforts to systematically and continuously have the accomplishments of Black people taught in the school systems. In 1915, he organized the "Association for the Study of Negro Life and History" and, in 1916, started the "Journal of Negro History". In 1926, he initiated the observance of "Negro History Week" which was later expanded to "Black History Month". Dr. Woodson felt that any African American only exposed to the White educational system without any exposure to positive Black achievements was "mis-educated and completely useless to his race."

The founding of the "Association for the Study of Negro Life and History" in 1915 was one of Woodson's most important accomplishments. Centered in Washington D.C., this association gathered as many books on Black history and achievements as possible and many of these books were later used as textbooks in all grades of schools, from elementary to the university. Dr. Woodson also published voluminously to help fill the initial textbook void. His most popular books include: A Century of Negro Education; History of the Negro Church; The Rural Negro; Education of the Negro Prior to 1861; Mis-Education of the Negro; African Backgrounds Outlined; African Heroes and Heroines; and The Negro in Our History. Dr. Woodson also collected vast quantities of original documents by people of African descent, which might otherwise have been lost.

Dr. Woodson's "Journal of Negro History" soon became established as one of the most scholarly and authoritative journals in America. The journal received contributions from some of America's foremost scholars, both Black and White, with many of its articles widely quoted in the leading educational centers of Europe, Asia, Africa, Latin America, and the United States. Woodson hoped that articles from his journal would help Black students develop a more self-respecting view of themselves. J.A. Rogers says: "Woodson's outspokenness at the manner in which Negroes were being taught to despise themselves by their teachers brought him several powerful enemies among leading Negro educators; but undaunted, he attacked them fearlessly until they were forced to his point of view."

"Negro History Week" was initiated in 1926, with Carter G. Woodson as the principal founder. "Negro History Week" forced both Black and White schools and colleges throughout the nation to gather and present information on "Negro" history and achievements, which they had never done before. Woodson once said at the annual meeting of the Georgia Teachers' and Educational Association: "I lament the teachers' ignorance of their rich heritage...Few of our college presidents could make more than 10% on an examination in Negro history."

Dr. Woodson was extremely critical of the so-called "highly educated"; that is, "the Negroes who have put on the finishing touches of our best colleges." He

Historian and educator Carter Goodwin Woodson pioneered the study and teaching of African-American history.

wrote: "The same educational process which inspires and stimulates the oppressor with the thought that he is everything and has accomplished everything worthwhile, depresses and crushes at the same time the spark of genius in the Negro by making him feel that his race does not amount to much and never will measure up to the standards of other peoples. The Negro thus educated is a hopeless liability of the race." Woodson frequently told his audiences that it took him over 20 years to "get over" his Harvard education. He felt "modern education" meant bringing a person's mind under the control of his oppressor. He wrote that once a Black person's mind is controlled, you won't have to tell him to go to the back door because he will already know his "proper place". He continued: " In fact, if there is no back door, he will cut one out for his special benefit. His education makes it necessary."

Dr. Woodson had even less respect for the Black professional class, believing it to be more culturally backward and less race conscious than the masses. In 1930, he analyzed 25,000 Black professionals, including doctors, dentists, and lawyers, and concluded that they were more interested in making money than contributing to the advancement of their professions or to their race. He wrote that Black professionals were less likely than their White counterparts to keep up with the professional literature in their fields, and that Black professional associations tended to emphasize social rather than professional advancement. Although Black professionals were dependent upon the Black working class to earn a living, Woodson saw the Black professional as "just as much class prejudice against the poor Negro as his White professional counterpart" and the least socially responsible among all Black people. Woodson viewed the Black physician as the worst. He wrote that "Black physicians, when attending meetings of the National Medical Association, were more interested in discussing the merits or demerits of the latest Cadillac than discussing the proper treatment for Tuberculosis or Typhoid Fever." He said that most successful Black physicians "frittered away much of their energy in quest of material things like fine cars, fine homes, and a fine time." Woodson once told a group of professionals: "You spend millions yearly to straighten your hair and bleach your skin and some of you go so far as to have your noses lifted in the hope of looking like the White man. Well, monkeys too have straight hair and thin lips."

Dr. Carter Goodwin Woodson was born on December 19, 1875, in New Canton, Virginia, to parents who were former slaves. Woodson was the eldest of nine children and was forced to work in the coalmines of West Virginia at an early age to help his parents make ends meet. This precluded his attending school until he was twenty years old. However, his love of knowledge was so great that despite the hard work he studied by himself at night and was especially fond of Greek and Latin classics. When he finally was able to go to school, he scored so high on the high school entrance examination that he was given an advanced standing and thus earned a diploma in only 18 months. Woodson then went on to obtain his bachelor's degree and master's degree at the University of Chicago. He completed studies for his Ph.D. at Harvard University in 1912, and then went to Sorbonne, Paris, where he was one of the most brilliant students in "French languages and literature" for that year. After teaching several years in West Virginia, he went to the Philippines as a teacher, and five months later was promoted to "Supervisor of Education" where he served for three years. He subsequently returned to the United States to become dean of the School of Liberal Arts at Howard University and later, dean of the West Virginia Collegiate Institute.

Carter Goodwin Woodson would be proud to know that Black history is now a well-established, legitimate, and respected subject of study, and that historians are finally acknowledging his pioneering contributions. Dr. Woodson was tremendously effective in helping to improve the self-respect of Black people and giving them a brighter, more optimistic outlook. As he so eloquently said: "If you read the history of Africa, the history of your ancestors–people of whom you should feel proud–you will realize that they have a history that is worthwhile. They have traditions that have value of which you can boast and upon which you can base a claim for the right to share in the blessings of democracy."

REFERENCES AND ADDITIONAL READING

Adams, R. (1969) <u>Great Negroes Past and Present.</u> Chicago: Afro-Am Publishing Co.

Bennett, L. (1988) <u>Before the Mayflower: A History of Black America</u>. New York: Penguin Books.

Bontemps, A. (1972) <u>Harlem Renaissance Remembered.</u> New York: Dodd Mead.

Clarke, J. (ed.) <u>Harlem: A Community in Transition</u>. New York: Citadel Press.

Goggin, J. (1993) <u>Carter G. Woodson: A Life in Black History.</u> Baton Rouge: Louisiana State University Press.

Gubert, B. (1982) <u>Early Black Bibliographies, 1863-1918</u>. New York: R.R. Garland Publishing.

Huggins, N. (1971) <u>Harlem Renaissance.</u> New York: Oxford University Press.

Rogers, J. (1972) <u>World's Great Men of Color</u>. New York: Macmillan Publishing Co.

Salley, C. (1993) <u>The Black 100: A Ranking of the Most Influential African-Americans Past and Present</u>. New York: Carol Publishing Group.

Smith, J. (1977) <u>Black Academic Libraries and Research Collections: An Historical Survey</u>. Westport, Conn.: Greenwood Press.

Thorpe, E. (1971) <u>Black Historians: A Critique</u>. New York: William Morow.

Woodson, C. (1990) <u>The Mis-Education of the Negro</u>. Trenton, NJ: Africa World Press Inc.

BLACKS IN THE MILITARY

Television images of General Colin Powell in specific, and Black, well trained, energetic soldiers in general are a great source of pride for most African Americans. These television images represent the fruits of over 200 years of struggle by African Americans for equality, integration, and respect in the military service. There is probably no irony in American history more pointed than the American Black soldier fighting and dying for basic American democracy and freedom, while being denied most of those same freedoms at home and in the military since the founding of this country.

General Colin Powell

Christian Fleetwood with Medal of Honor

Until recently African Americans begged for the privilege to fight and die for this country in hopes that a more equitable society would await them at the end of the war. However, Black soldiers and sailors were strictly prohibited from participation in virtually every American war until a severe manpower shortage made this country desperate. In 1792, laws were passed by Congress to exclude Blacks from the Army and Marines. The Marine Corp did not accept an African American for its first 150 years of existence, up to and including World War II, when White politicians and generals finally became desperate enough to encourage Black military participation. Black soldiers were frequently poorly trained, unequally paid and equipped, and forced to participate in all Black regiments with White Southern officers in charge.

Robert Smalls stole the Confederate gunboat "Planter" out of Charleston Harbor on May 13, 1862 and delivered it to the Union.

When Blacks were allowed to participate in American wars, they invariably performed exceptionally well. Over 5,000 African Americans, both slave and free, served in the army during the Revolutionary War, and almost all of them received their freedom in appreciation after the war. In fact, most Northern states abolished slavery because of their contribution. The outstanding contributions of over 200,000 African American soldiers and sailors during the Civil War led to the 13th Amendment freeing all slaves.

Between 1869 and 1890, Black soldiers in the West, nicknamed the Buffalo Soldiers, won 14 Congressional Medals of Honor, 9 Certificates of Merit, and 29 Orders of Honorable Mention, while fighting Native Americans. President Theodore Roosevelt credited these same Buffalo Soldiers for saving his famous "Rough Riders" from extermination in Cuba during the Spanish American War of 1898.

Buffalo Soldiers

World War I Poster

About 160,000 of the 200,000 African Americans sent to Europe during World War I were forced to work as laborers in unloading ships and building roads. The remaining soldiers were not even allowed to fight alongside White American soldiers, but rather were assigned by General Pershing to French Divisions. These Black soldiers had to fight in French uniforms with French weapons and French leadership until the end of World War I. Over 3,000 casualties were sustained by these Black soldiers, who subsequently were awarded over 540 medals by the French government including the Legion of Honor-for gallantry in action.

The plight of Blacks in the military did not improve significantly until President Franklin Roosevelt and President Harry Truman made concessions to Black leaders in exchange for Black votes. On October 15, 1940, Roosevelt announced that Blacks would be trained as pilots, that Black reserve officers would be called to active duty, and that Colonel Benjamin Davis would be named the first Black brigadier general.

In 1948, Truman was even more desperate for Black votes and issued Executive Order 9981, ending military segregation and demanding "equality of treatment and opportunity for all persons in the Armed Services without regard to race, color, religion or national origin." After 200 years of struggle, African Americans can now look upon Black military men and officers with a great sense of pride and accomplishment.

REFERENCES AND ADDITIONAL READING

Donaldson, G. (1991) <u>The History of African-Americans in the Military</u>. Malabar, FL: Krieger Publishing Co.

Foner, J. (1974) <u>Blacks and the Military in American History</u>. New York: A New Perspective Publishing Co.

Greene, R. (1974) <u>Black Defenders of America: 1775-1973</u>. Chicago: Johnson Publishing.

Langley, H. (1967) <u>Social Reforms in the United States Navy: 1798-1862</u>. Urbana, IL: University of Illinois Press.

Lanning, M. (1997) <u>The African-American Soldier From Crispus Attucks to Colin Powell</u>. Secaucus, NJ: Carol Publishing Group.

Moebs, T. (1994) <u>Black Soldiers-Black Sailors-Black Ink: Research Guide on African - Americans in U.S. Military History</u>. Chesapeake Bay, MD: Moebs Publishing Co.

Mullen, R. (1973) <u>Blacks in America's Wars</u>. New York: Pathfinder.

Nalty, B. (1986) <u>Strength for the Fight: A History of Black Americans in the Military.</u> New York: Free Press.

Rogers, J. (1989) <u>Africa's Gift to America.</u> St. Petersburg, FL: Helga Rogers Publishing.

Wilson, J. (1977) <u>The Black Phalanx: A History of the Negro Soldier of the United States in the Wars of 1775-1812, 1861-1865</u>. New York: Arno Press.

Zinn, H. (1980) <u>A People's History of the United States</u>. New York: HarperCollins Publishers.

WORLD WAR II ATROCITIES AND BLACK SERVICEMEN

Most Americans would never believe that the United States government was involved in atrocities. After all, does not the U.S. currency have "IN GOD WE TRUST" written all over it. Moreover, most Americans still do not believe that the U.S. government funded a "NO TREATMENT" syphilis study in Tuskegee, Alabama for 40 years or that hundreds of Vietnamese were massacred at "My Lai". Authors Carroll Case (<u>The Slaughter</u>) and Robert Allen (<u>The Port Chicago Mutiny</u>) have written even less believable stories about the U.S. Military's treatment towards Blacks.

Most Black servicemen were only allowed to load ammunition during World War II.

Black servicemen found life exceptionally difficult during World War II. Racism was rampant, segregation made everything separate and extremely unequal, and opportunities for advancement for Blacks were non-existent. In fact, Black servicemen were considered "inferior and ill qualified" according to an Army War College committee study in 1940, that also concluded that Blacks were "far below the Whites in capacity to absorb instruction." Initially, the Army assigned Black soldiers to labor and support units, and the Navy made Black sailors either messman waiting tables, or ammunition loaders. African American servicemen were not allowed into combat until manpower shortages became severe. In fact, General Patton vehemently refused to allow any Blacks to serve under his command under any circumstances. Despite legendary acts of heroism which often cost their lives, not a single Black person received the Medal of Honor during World War II, and Lieutenant General (retired) William McCaffrey says the reason was simple: "Everyone in the Army then was a racist." Fifty years later the Department of Defense decided that seven Black soldiers deserved the Medal of Honor. On January 13, 1997, President Clinton presented the Medal of Honor to the only survivor, Vernon Baker, and to the families of the others stating: "They were denied their nation's highest honor, but their deeds could not be denied."

African American servicemen were severely punished for military and civil crimes and rarely received a fair trial under military justice. All but three of the 21 American soldiers executed for capital crimes during World War II were Black. The Army hung six African Americans after a hastily conducted military police investigation accused them of raping a White nurse in New Guinea. The soldiers went to their deaths proclaiming their innocence. Brigadier General Benjamin Davis made an inspection tour of army camps throughout the United States in 1943, and concluded: "There is still great dissatisfaction on the part of the Colored soldier. The War Department offers him nothing but humiliation and mistreatment and has even introduced Jim Crow practices in areas, both at home and abroad, where they have not hitherto been practiced." African American anger and frustration with lack of opportunity and discrimination resulted in numerous work stoppages and riots. For example, in 1944 Black sailors rioted after racial harassment from White Marines on the island of Guam turned violent. Black soldiers of the 364th infantry also rioted in Phoenix, Arizona for alleged mistreatment. In March 1945, members of a Black construction battalion at Port Hueneme, California, protested nonviolently against their White commander's racism by refusing to eat for two days.

Carroll Case in <u>The Slaughter</u> claims the worse military atrocity occurred at Camp Van Dorn in southern Mississippi in 1943, where over 1,200 Black soldiers of the 364th infantry were murdered with machine guns by White military police. Although the Army has no record of this incident, Case says he has thousands of sworn affidavits from eyewitnesses, including one of the military police involved in the shooting. The fate of the 364th was sealed after racial violence erupted in Phoenix, Arizona on Thanksgiving night in 1942, according to Carroll Case. Approximately one hundred men took part in a shootout with a detachment of White military police resulting in fifteen casualties. Inspector General Peterson labeled this incident as "having all the earmarks of a mutiny." Sixteen men of the 364th were tried by general court martial and sentenced to fifty years hard labor. As punishment, the remaining members of the 364th were sent to Fort Van Dorn, an extremely racist base near Centerville, Mississippi.

Even the sidewalks were segregated in Centerville, Mississippi, and the "uppity" 364th outraged the citizens by demanding equal treatment. On Sunday May 30, 1944, an MP stopped a soldier and ordered him back to base, because a button on his uniform was missing. When the soldier objected, the local sheriff shot and killed the soldier and asked the MP if "any other Nigger needed killing." After word of the soldier's death reached the base, riots ensued that resulted in the death of 25 additional Black soldiers. There is no official documentation of either incident according to Case, but several soldiers wrote letters detailing the events. Another major disturbance occurred one month later involving 3,000 soldiers and the 99th Infantry Division had to be called to stop the violence. Carroll Case says the Army then ordered the 364th quarantined to their barracks, where later that night, White MPs slaughtered them with machine guns. The bodies were loaded in boxcars and taken to the south gate of the base, where they were dumped into a large bulldozed trench. Case says all records after this blood bath were destroyed, but that he has even interviewed men in the laundry room, who remembered receiving the blood soaked linen from the barracks.

Train to Mississippi

Port Chicago was a naval ammunition base located about 30 miles from San Francisco, on the Sacramento River. The ammunition depot at Port Chicago was one of the main sources of supply for the Pacific fleet because the dock facilities could handle the largest ammunition carriers in the Navy. All of the men who actually handled the ammunition and bombs were Black, and all of the commissioned officers were White. Explosives were transferred from boxcars to ship holds 24 hours a day, and the work was hard and dangerous. Some ships received over 8,500 tons of ammunition and bombs.

Black sailors complained that neither they, nor their officers, had received any training in handling the explosives. They felt the explosives were dangerous and needed better supervision. When the Coast Guard inspected the port and complained about unsafe practices, they were asked to leave. The naval officers told the Black sailors that the bombs could never explode because the firing pins and fuses had been removed. On July 17, 1944, a gigantic explosion estimated equivalent to a five-kiloton atomic bomb, instantly killed 202 Black ammunition loaders and destroyed two cargo ships. The small town of Port Chicago, and the base itself, both over a mile away, were severely damaged. This was by far the worst home-front disaster of World War II. A subsequent naval investigation held the Black sailors 100% responsible for the explosion, citing rough ammunition handling.

When Port Chicago was rebuilt, fifty sailors refused to return to ammunition loading, because of inadequate training and a lack of safety provisions for hazardous duty. The 50 sailors were convicted of mutiny, sentenced to fifteen years hard labor and received dishonorable discharges. Not until after the war, January 1946, was future Supreme Court Justice Thurgood Marshall able to appeal the verdict and influence the Navy to return the men to active duty. The mutiny convictions however, were never removed from their records. In May 1998, several Black Congressmen made a written appeal to President Clinton to reverse the mutiny convictions and clear the names of these courageous men.

Port Chicago:View from the South

Port Chicago:View from the North

Even more intriguing is the current belief that the Port Chicago explosion was not an accident at all. Many claim to have irrefutable evidence that the U.S. military used Port Chicago to evaluate the damage of an atomic bomb delivered by ship and concluded that air explosions would produce far more destruction. Navy pilots in the area claim to have seen a Wilson condensation ring and mushroom cloud, which are seen only after an atomic bomb detonation. The atomic bombs under consideration were called Mark I (little boy), Mark II, and Mark III (fat boy). Mark II was allegedly tested on the hapless souls at Port Chicago and abandoned because the damage radius was inadequate. Subsequently, the two atomic bombs destined for Japan (Mark I and Mark III) were delivered to an island near Port Chicago and loaded onto B-29 bombers for aerial delivery.

In 1948, President Truman needed the Black vote and consequently decided to "do the right thing" and conclude his presidency in an "honorable way". On July 26, 1948, Truman issued executive order 9981 which declared: "...there shall be equality of treatment and opportunity for all persons in the armed forces without regard to race, color, religion, or national origin." Perhaps the American government should also "do the right thing" and acknowledge and apologize for the numerous atrocities, during World War II, involving Black servicemen.

Thurgood Marshall

Was Port Chicago an
Atomic Test Site?

REFERENCES AND ADDITIONAL READING

Allen, R. (1993) <u>The Port Chicago Mutiny</u>. New York: Amistad Press Inc.

Buchanan, A. (1972) <u>Black Americans in World War II.</u> Santa Barbara, CA.

Case, C. (1998) <u>The Slaughter: An American Atrocity</u>. Mississippi: FBC Inc.

Donaldson, G. (1991) <u>The History of African-Americans in the Military.</u> Malabar, FL: Krieger Publishing Co.

Foner, J. (1974) <u>Blacks and the Military in American History.</u> New York: A New Perspective Publishing Co.

Lanning, M. (1997) <u>The African-American Soldier From Crispus Attucks to Colin Powell</u>. Secaucus, NJ: Carol Publishing Group.

Moebs, T. (1994) <u>Black Soldiers-Black Sailors-Black Ink: Research Guide on African - Americans in U.S. Military History</u>. Chesapeake Bay, MD: Moebs Publishing Co.

Mullen, R. (1973) <u>Blacks in America's Wars</u>. New York: Pathfinder.

Nalty, B. (1986) <u>Strength for the Fight: A History of Black Americans in the Military</u>. New York: Free Press.

Pearson, R. (1964) <u>No Share of Glory</u>. Pacific Palisades, CA.

Zinn, H. (1980) <u>A People's History of the United States.</u> New York: HarperCollins Publishers.

BLACK NATIONALISM

Black Nationalism is defined as "a complex set of beliefs emphasizing the need for the cultural, political, and economic separation of African Americans from White society." The philosophy of Black Nationalism is a direct response to racial discrimination and the overt hostility of White society toward anyone of African descent. Black Nationalist beliefs were strongest during slavery and again with Marcus Garvey at the beginning of the 20th century. Since most Black Nationalists believed that White society would never treat African Americans fairly, they demanded a territorial base either in Africa or in America, completely governed by Black men.

Black Panthers Bobby Seale and Huey Newton

As the philosophy of Black Nationalism expanded, Black pride, solidarity, and self-reliance became issues just as important as the demand for a territorial base. For example, in the 18th century, Boston's free Blacks demanded that Crispus Attucks, the first to die in the American Revolution, become a symbol of African American contributions to the Revolutionary War. Crispus Attucks Day (March 5) was celebrated for decades before it was replaced by July 4th. During the 19th century, Paul Cuffe, the richest Black man in America, employed only African Americans to demonstrate their ability to the skeptical White world. In the 1920s, Marcus Garvey demanded distinctly Black standards of beauty and refused any advertisements in his newspaper "The Negro World" for hair straighteners or skin Whiteners. He insisted on highlighting the accomplishments of Blacks throughout the world and that Black people chose Black heroes. He even demanded that Black churches depict all religious figures as Black, including Jesus Christ.

Malcolm X

During the Civil Rights Movement of the 1960s, many young Blacks became impatient with its slow progress and passive non-violent philosophy and again embraced Black Nationalism. Stokely Carmichael (Kwame Ture) and the Student Nonviolent Coordinating Committee (SNCC) soon had most Black youths proclaiming the slogans "Black is Beautiful" and "Black Power". Bobby Seale and Huey Newton founded the "Black Panther Party" in 1966, and advocated militant self defense in addition to Black Nationalism. Elijah Muhammad (a former Garveyite) and Malcolm X emphasized religious justification for racially separate enterprises, especially in business. When the young Black leaders of the Civil Rights Movement looked for the "Father of Black Nationalism", they chose a name that history had almost forgotten: Martin Robison Delany.

Martin Robison Delany (1812-1885) was a highly intelligent, well-educated Black Nationalist with an immense and outspoken love for his people. Delany strenuously rejected the notion of Black inferiority and proposed emigration rather than the continuous submission to racial humiliation by White society. Although

Martin Robison Delany

his father, Samuel Delany, was a slave, Martin was born free because his mother Pati Peace Delany, was free. The Delany children mastered reading and education so quickly that West Virginian Whites became threatened and forced them into Pennsylvania, in 1822. In 1831, Martin completed the Reverend Lewis Woodson School for Negroes and later completed enough medical study in the offices of abolitionist medical doctors to make a comfortable living as a medical practitioner. In 1850, he became the first Black admitted to Harvard Medical School but was asked to leave after one year because Dean Oliver Holmes considered him a "distraction to education".

Martin Delany hated slavery and while still practicing medicine, he published the "Mystery", the first Black-owned newspaper "West of the Alleghenies". He published his abolitionist newspaper from 1843-47 and when finances forced him to close, he joined Frederick Douglass as coeditor of the newly founded "North Star". Delany demanded liberty for Blacks as a human right. He also exhorted Blacks to elevate themselves by becoming skilled workers and landowning farmers.

Martin Delany emphasized Black self-reliance through education, independent thought, and self respect. He felt that Blacks would only gain "the world's applause" by obtaining wealth through successful businesses.

When Congress passed the Fugitive Slave Act, Delany gave up all hope that this country would ever ameliorate the condition of his people. He moved his family to Canada and became a full time advocate for emigration to Africa. Delany organized three emigration conventions (in 1854, 1856, and 1858). In July 1859, Martin Delany sailed to Western Africa and on December 27, 1859, he signed a treaty with the king of Abeokuta (Nigeria). The treaty "permitted African Americans associated with Delany to settle in unused tribal lands in exchange for sharing their skills and education with the Yoruba people." Happy with his African treaty, Delany then sailed for Britain to obtain financial support.

In London, Martin Delany was able to convince cotton dealers and philanthropists that Christian colonies in Africa could easily compete with slave cotton from the South. Delany helped found the "African Aid Society", which agreed to lend two thirds of the money needed by the first group of settlers who were expected to leave the U.S. in June 1861. Unfortunately, before the first settlers could leave, the Civil War began, and Delany decided to cancel the first group's departure.

After four years of bloodshed, Martin Delany was able to convince President Lincoln to allow him to recruit an all Black army with Black officers, which would terrorize the South by arming all slaves and encouraging them to fight for their own emancipation. Delany was commissioned as a Major in the Union Army, the first Black field officer, but the war ended before he could implement his plan to arm all slaves. After the war, Delany was labeled as a "race agitator" for telling freed slaves to "trust only Blacks" and "to break the peace of society and force their way by insurrection to a position he is ambitious they should attain to."

African Methodist Episcopal Church (AME) Bishop Daniel Payne wrote that "Delany was too intensely African to be popular...had his love for humanity been as great as his love for his race, his influence might have equaled that of Fredrick Douglass." Martin Delany's emphasis on race pride and self-reliance and his stressing of the importance of "elevating the race" clearly makes him the "Father of Black Nationalism".

REFERENCES AND ADDITIONAL READING

Adams, R. (1969) Great Negroes: Past and Present. Chicago: Afro-Am Publishing Co. Inc.

Appiah, K. & Gates, H. (eds.) (1999) Africana. New York: Basis Civitas Books.

Asante, M. & Mattson, M. (1991) Historical and Cultural Atlas of African Americans. New York: Macmillan Publishing Co.

Bennett, L. (1988) Before the Mayflower. New York: Penguin Books.

Bennett, L. (1975) The Shaping of Black America. Chicago: Johnson Publishing Co.

Franklin, J. & Meier, A. (ed.) (1982) Black Leaders of the Twentieth Century. Chicago: University of Illinois Press.

Franklin, J. (1988) From Slavery to Freedom: A History of Negro Americans. New York: Alfred A. Knopf.

Griffith, C. (1975) The African Dream: Martin R. Delany and the Emergence of Pan-African Thought. University Park: Pennsylvania State University.

Litwack, L. & Meier, A. (1988) Black Leaders of the Nineteenth Century. Chicago: University of Illinois Press.Low, A. & Clift, V. (eds.) (1983) Encyclopedia of Black America. New York: Neal Schuman Publishers.

Moses, W. (ed.) (1996) Classical Black Nationalism: From American Revolution to Marcus Garvey. New York: New York University Press.

Moses, W. (1988) The Golden Age of Black Nationalism, 1850-1925. NewYork: Oxford University Press.

Sally C. (1993) The Black 100. New York: Carol Publishing Group.

PHOTOGRAPHIC CREDITS

I would like to sincerely thank the following people, publishers, organizations, and institutions for providing the photographs and illustrations present on the specified pages below in this book and for granting me permission to publish their material:

Library of Congress, Photoduplication service: pages 3, 21, 25, 26, 34, 35, 47, 52, 56, 60, 65, 68, 70, 74, 80, 91, 94, 98, 99, 110, 119, 120, 131, 142, 146, 150, 152, 156, 157, 160, 168, 169, 182, 183, 187, 201, 203, 208, 209, 225, 228, 235, 238, 240, 241.

The New York Public Library & Schomburg Center for Research in Black Culture: pages 24, 84, 86, 102, 110, 111, 114, 115, 122, 126, 129, 132, 138, 143, 144, 151, 161, 163, 173, 182, 194, 195, 196, 207, 214, 219, 221, 225, 238, 242.

Helga M. Rogers Publishing (Mrs. J. A. Rogers): pages 2, 5, 7, 8, 12, 13, 16, 17, 31, 40, 48, 57, 85, 90, 109, 136, 137, 138, 169, 209.

Department of the Navy / Naval Historical Center: pages 194, 226, 227, 228, 229, 232, 237.

National Archives and Records Administration: pages 23, 183, 188, 228,

Eakin Press and Mr. Hannibal Johnson: pages 202, 204, 205.

The Philadelphia Museum of Art, John G. Johnson Collection: page 43.

Mrs. Mary Lewis, graphic designer, re-drew C. A. Diop on page 21 and designed the beautiful cover.

ACKNOWLEDGEMENTS

These articles began as five-minute history lessons at the end of weekly newscasts on KPFK radio. Subsequently, the Los Angeles Sentinel newspaper agreed to publish these history articles weekly in a section entitled "Our African Heritage". I ameternally grateful to the Los Angeles Sentinel owner, editor, and staff (especially Mrs. Virgie Murray) for the gracious and genuinely heart-warming commentary provided by their readers and the friendships made as a result of these publications.

The final editorial corrections and comments for this book were provided by Ms. Sandra Moore and to her I am extremely thankful. I must also acknowledge the earlier editorial expertise provided during preparation of the newspaper articles by my wife, DeMetria, and my children Imana, Leroy Jr., Retina, and Renee. Imana went above and beyond the call of duty by establishing a Black history website with these articles at the exclusive Charlotte Country Day School in Charlotte, NC, where she teaches computer technology. More than a few questions about Egyptian ethnicity, etc., were directed to me from this website.

Procrastination may have prevented these articles from ever reaching book form without the constant prodding and demanding by Ms. J. Nayer Hardin of the Computer Underground Railroad that this information be widely disseminated among our young people, and adults, for their upliftment. Moreover, her contribution of preparing this material with desktop publisher required an enormous amount of work and commitment. I must also thank Mrs. Bobby Howe, and the owners of KTYM radio, for annually encouraging my participation as their Black history month expert, and for periodically airing these interviews throughout the year.

Finally, I am immensely grateful to professional graphic designer, Mrs. Mary Lewis, for providing the beautiful cover design, and for formatting the text and photographs throughout this book.

COPIES OF THIS BOOK MAY BE ORDERED FROM:

Dr. Leroy William Vaughn
323 North Prairie Avenue
Suite 217
Inglewood, CA 90301

Name _____

Address _____

City/State/Zip _____

<u>**BLACK PEOPLE AND THEIR PLACE IN WORLD HISTORY**</u> $17.00 each
    Shipping and Handling: 2.95

Please Make check or money order payable to: Dr. Leroy Vaughn

TO ORDER BY PHONE: 1-800-247-6553

TO ORDER ONLINE: http://www.atlasbooks.com

Willie "C" Jackson
1531 W. 64th Street
Los Angeles CA. 90047

Willie "C" Jackson
1531 W. 64th Street
Los Angeles CA. 90047